WHISPERS OF BECOMING

A MEMOIR

VANESSA DELGADO

VANESSA DELGADO

WHISPERS OF BECOMING

CONTENTS

Prologue	1
Chapter 1	5
A Fateful Encounter	
Chapter 2	12
Cinnamon Secrets: A Grandmother's Love Brewed	
Chapter 3	14
New Beginnings	
Chapter 4	19
Rekindling Distant Bonds	
Chapter 5	22
Silent Echoes of a Father's Absence	
Chapter 6	31
Hidden Struggles of Senior Year	
Chapter 7	37
From Shadows to Strength	
Chapter 8	48
Finding Balance in Chaos	
Chapter 9	61
Packing Up and Moving On	
Chapter 10	72
Rock Bottom Comeback	
Chapter 11	78
From Survival to Self-Discovery	
Chapter 12	82
Leaving Home	
Chapter 13	87
Journey of Healing	
Chapter 14	93
Healing Through Boundaries	
Chapter 15	97
Anxiety and Connection	
Chapter 16	104
Cycles of Growth and Setback	
Chapter 17	110
Breaking Free from Pleasing Others	

Afterword	113
Resources & Recommendations	115

Copyright © 2025 by Vanessa Delgado

All rights reserved.

No part of this book may be reproduced, stored in a retrieval system, or transmitted in any form or by any means—electronic, mechanical, photocopying, recording, or otherwise—without the prior written permission of the publisher, except in the case of brief quotations embodied in critical articles or reviews.

Printed by Ingramspark.

ISBN: 979-8-9906832-1-1

This is a work of nonfiction. Names and identifying details have been kept private to protect the privacy of individuals.

Any resemblance to actual persons, living or dead, is purely coincidental.

Credits

Editor: Stephanie Wilson

Printed in the United States of America

First edition

 Formatted with Vellum

PROLOGUE

This isn't a story of overnight success or a life lived neatly in order. It's a story of survival, of mess, of broken cycles and hard truths. It's a story of sitting on the bathroom floor with tears streaming down my face, asking God if He was even listening. Of walking into gyms terrified, of chasing perfection in the mirror, of unraveling family wounds that shaped me in ways I didn't yet understand.

For much of my life, I believed love had to be earned. That if I looked the part, achieved enough, or stayed quiet enough, maybe I'd be chosen. Maybe I'd finally be enough. But that belief only left me exhausted, anxious, and disconnected from who I really was.

This book isn't about perfection. It's about healing, about making mistakes, about learning to stop shrinking and finally take up space. It's about what happens when you stop surviving and start asking for more.

If you've ever felt like too much, or not enough—sometimes

both in the same breath—then maybe you'll see pieces of yourself here. I don't have all the answers, but I do have this: the story of how I've been learning, slowly and painfully, to love myself anyway.

To the little girl inside me who only wanted to be seen and loved - this is for you.

To my mother, whose struggles became my lessons, and whose healing journey has intertwined with mine.

To the broken pieces of myself that refused to give up, even when it felt impossible.

And to you, the reader—especially if you've ever felt like too much or not enough. May these pages remind you that you are not alone, and that healing, in all its mess and beauty, is possible.

CHAPTER ONE

A FATEFUL ENCOUNTER

It was a chilly winter evening in 2017 when I came home from the gym, exhausted and ready to shower. As I reached into my closet for my pajamas, the two full-length mirrors on the doors caught my eye. For a moment, I stopped.

What I saw in the reflection startled and saddened me. It was the first time I had truly looked at myself since going through a "pretend prep cut" months earlier. My body was worn down. My hair was falling out. My menstrual cycle had been gone for nearly four months.

As I stared back at my own reflection, something in my eyes took me even further back — to high school, when I had attempted suicide. The look staring back at me was the same: self-hatred and shame. The same look I had carried three years earlier, at my heaviest weight. When I stood there, pinching at my love handles, calling myself a "fat bitch." It was a cruel, familiar ritual. But in that instant, something was different.

For the first time, after countless moments of self-deprecation, I realized I couldn't keep going down this path any longer.

Something loosened inside me then — a raw swell of sadness and a quick flash of anger that felt like a verdict: I needed to know why. It wasn't about calories or the fit of my jeans; it felt older, as if something had been pulling at me for years. I pressed my palm to the cool glass and the room shrank to one stubborn question: where did this come from? It wasn't curiosity so much as a demand. If I wanted to change anything, I realized, I had to go back farther than my own choices — back to the night that made me possible, to what my mother and father did and didn't say, to the small inheritances passed down without anyone naming them. I closed the closet and started looking for the beginning.

ALTHOUGH MY MOTHER had briefly shared bits and pieces of her story before, I've sat with her many times during my adult healing journey to reflect more deeply on her memory. My mothers version of what happened all started when she was just 13 working at a locally owned Italian ice and food drive in Illinois. By the time she turned 14, whispers floated around about a young man showing interest in her. She remembered, these rumors were vague and lacking in detail, so she dismissed them without much thought. She was vaguely familiar with this guy, having seen him in passing. However, it wasn't until about a year later that she noticed his presence more frequently. He seemed to pop up at her school, linger near the city bus stops, and even appear at her workplace. Their first real conversation happened under unexpected circumstances. She had been invited to participate in a quinceañera as one of the damas. During one of the dance rehearsals, there was a sudden change—her original dance

CHAPTER ONE

partner was replaced with this man she'd been seeing around frequently. She found the switch curious but didn't dwell on it, focusing instead on learning the choreography.

My mother described by the age of 16, she found his persistent attention unsettling and felt a creeping fear. Desperately seeking reassurance, she confided in her mother, hoping for some guidance or comfort. Yet, the advice she received was perplexing: *"date him, but ignore him, and eventually, he will lose interest and move on to someone else".*

Torn between her instincts and her mother's counsel, my mother reluctantly tried to follow this unconventional advice. Their so-called "dating" was nothing like the norm, as they never actually went out together. She'd see him around, but most of their encounters were never alone. It was sudden when he proposed, but the proposal came with a threat—he demanded she marry him or face consequences. As they became engaged, he insisted she leave with him without explaining what that entailed. My mother recalled this left her in a state of confusion, unsure of what his intentions were or whether any of it was even real.

My mother said she told her mother more than once that she felt unsafe and didn't want him as a boyfriend, but she never received support. Each time she brought it up, her mother grew colder. My mother remembered one summer day she would never forget —

August 1987

She was walking on her way to work when she faintly heard her name being called. She didn't recognize the voice. The moment she tried to turn to see where the voice came from, someone reached over and covered her mouth and pushed her into a blue Chevy car. The man was her soon to be husband; who told her to stay down so one could see her.

She recalled the drive had to be over an hour, this whole time my mother was down in the seat remaining a quiet ride and my mother afraid and confused. Suddenly he said to himself out loud *"Where are we going, we are going back"*. At that moment he allowed her to sit up normally. It seemed like he was driving through the back roads from what my mother could tell.

They ended up at a man's house, and that's when she realized where they were, a town not too far from where they lived. My mothers - soon to be husband spoke to a man who came out and got into his own car while my mothers 'fiancé' followed him into what kept only surprising my mother as they arrived at a nearby motel. The man passed the keys over and drove off, while my mother and her 'fiancé' walked into the motel room.

The day was growing dark, when my mothers 'fiancé' told my mother she couldn't leave. He left shortly after they arrived at the motel for several hours. Upon his return, she instantly noticed markings on his neck and a brown paper bag that he walked into the bathroom with. He came out from the bathroom, turned off the light and lay on one of the 2 full size beds. My mother lay in the other bed, naive and afraid of the whole situation. As he got into the bed, he called my mother over to the bed with him. When she refused, he called her again with no options. That night was a violation — the moment she lost the choice over her own body.

CHAPTER ONE

MY MOTHER'S version was compact and clipped. After a few days in a motel, he showed her a half-furnished apartment and said this would be their new home. She learned she was pregnant right away, and she also mentioned the beatings started then and kept coming. He kept her from her family until she stopped eating to force a reaction from him. When she finally told my grandmother and my aunt one day about her pregnancy after their visit was ending, my grandmother's answer was blunt: "*You can't count on me.*" My mother told the story quickly, as if stepping over stones; the things she didn't say were the ones that landed hardest.

My mother told me that after a couple of months she was allowed to go back to work at the Italian food and ice cream shop. By then the abuse had escalated; he began taking the gun out during certain altercations. She described the pregnancy as a time of fear and pain. Over the years she would give me fragments—short sentences, careful silences. I learned to step lightly around them; I didn't want to reopen things she had closed. Still, what she did tell me cut deep. She confessed, once, that she had tried to induce a miscarriage. Hearing that as her child made me feel small and ashamed in ways I couldn't explain. That admission became a weight I carried for years.

My mother recalled the violence, changed everything—how she moved through the house, how she moved me. At first she would put me somewhere safe; later she held on to me, hoping my presence would stop him. She told me my father aimed for the parts of her body that were furthest from me. As I grew older and became more mobile, my mother noticed a pattern during these moments of violence. She said she looked for me in a panic after my father had left, only to find me cowering in various hiding spots - behind the couch, under the table, or in the safety of a closet. These were my hiding places, where I sought refuge from the chaos and fear that consumed our home.

Those hiding places held the residue of fear—and in the spaces between, my mother fought to create calm. My mother carved out a small island of normal when he left for work—feed, bathe, pillows and cartoons. She'd settle me on the couch with stuffed animals surrounding me while I sat quietly. Despite being just a toddler, my mother was surprised at how well-behaved I was during these moments on the couch, she shared.

I WAS MY FATHERS SHADOW. The second he came home he would scoop me up and hold me tightly. He liked to feed me chopped french fries—McDonald's or Burger King—carefully counting each bite. I cried until he let me sleep on the bed next to him because being close felt like being held away from everything scary. It took me years to understand that the same arms that held me tight could also break the quiet of our home. The man who made those moments safe was the same one who could turn the house into a battlefield. Those small moments of normal could not hide the pattern for long. My mother tried to tell the family what was happening, but no one believed her. She had tried to leave three times; each time he found a way to bring her back. The first person who listened was the owner at her job. My mother shared one afternoon, when the owner asked if something was wrong, my mother finally told the truth. The woman believed her and promised to help—she said her daughter worked for an attorney and would arrange a meeting. At the attorney's office, as my mother told her story, the lawyer stopped her and named it: rape and kidnapping. The words hit like ice—

CHAPTER ONE

things my mother had lived through but never had names for, only a fog of blame and shame that had kept her silent. That was when she began to plan on leaving. Slowly and quietly she gathered clothes and small belongings and picked a day to go while he was at work. She called one of her brothers to come for her and to help collect what she had hidden away. When the papers finally arrived, the promise of legal action held a brittle, fragile power. My father came to my grandparents' house with divorce papers and a gun. My mother's jaw set; my grandmother's face folded from disbelief into aching belief. Hearing her tell it, I felt the strange double edge of that day — the cruelty of what had come before and the sharp relief of being believed at last. Relief did not erase what we had lived through, but it changed what could happen next. By the end of that summer we were not yet free of the long shadows he'd cast, but the shape of our days began to shift. I learned that safety could be made in small acts — a bag quietly packed, a phone call that reached someone who listened, a couch propped with pillows and cartoons. I also learned that memory keeps its own map: hiding places remembered, a mother's steady hands, and the weight of words finally spoken. The house was quieter in some ways and different in others; the fear that had once filled it had been named, and that naming opened a path for us to walk away.

CHAPTER TWO

CINNAMON SECRETS: A GRANDMOTHER'S LOVE BREWED

When my mother left my father, we moved into my grandparents' small house that summer. The familiar walls and creaky floors were a constant reminder of my mother's childhood home. My mother and I shared an unfinished basement as our bedroom, with only a thin curtain for privacy. But it was the open front porch that held the fondest memories. My grandmother would sit in the warm summer evenings, rocking back and forth in her wooden chair, cradling me in her arms. The scent of freshly cooked meals would cover the entire house, signaling that dinner was almost ready. I remember the porch first as a place of small comforts. At first, I struggled with the separation and missed my father terribly. I would cry and ask when we were going back home. Slowly, with the love and steady presence of my grandparents and three uncles who still lived with them, I began to adapt. They became my family and my safety net in small, practical ways — extra plates at the table and someone to teach me how to tie my shoes. My earliest memories of my grandmother are filled with warmth. She knew how to make oatmeal that tasted like it took hours to cook. She boiled water with whole cinnamon sticks, let the oats simmer to perfection, and — instead of a bowl — poured it into a sippy cup so I could carry it around. Cooking was one of her greatest talents; she showed affection that way, in food and in the small favors she did. Those daily rituals made me feel seen. But those small comforts sat beside harsher moments. She sometimes said things that cut — lines like, "*Your father/mother don't care about you; that's why they leave you here with me.*" Because she was someone I trusted, the words landed and replayed themselves in my head like a cassette stuck on repeat; whenever I felt ignored, the tape started again, and over time the confusion turned to anger. My grandmother was both shelter and a wound. She held me, fed me, and bought me small treasures, and she also said things that left marks. I don't know if she meant to hurt me. Memory keeps her both ways — and maybe that's the truest way to remember someone.

CHAPTER THREE

NEW BEGINNINGS

When I was five my mother finally found an apartment and we moved out of my grandparents' house. The ground-floor unit was cozy; one window looked out at towering trees, the other at a tall cement wall. The apartment arrived empty. Her first purchase was a bed for herself, and it took months for her to gather the rest of what she needed before she could bring me to live with her.

During that time I stayed with my grandparents. My uncles—who felt like big brothers—were around all the time and kept me company. Even though my mother tried to ease my worries, I couldn't shake the feeling that my parents didn't care about me. That belief lingered until she was able to provide more consistently.

When I moved in, my first bed was a black water bed that made me feel like I was floating on clouds. My room filled slowly: toys arrived, a shelf of books my mother collected for me, and a window sill lined with the collectible McDonald's Happy Meal toys from the

CHAPTER THREE

90s. Disney Princess sheets and matching curtains made my bed feel like a little castle. In my closet there were clothes galore and bins that were constantly being filled with board games and Barbies.

MY MOTHER MOVED QUICKLY to establish structure. She set a bedtime I never dared argue with—rules and routine gave me a predictability I didn't know how to ask for. She bought me a yellow cow stuffed-animal alarm clock so I could wake myself once I had shown her I wanted to do more for myself. When I started first grade, those small responsibilities mattered in a new way: learning to wake up on my own, choosing my own snacks, coming home ready to sit down with homework. We would go grocery shopping every week, carefully choosing snacks and breakfast foods to pack in my lunch. On Fridays I looked forward to visiting my grandparents after school.

There weren't many openly tender moments to point to; what she built for me was practical and ordered. But the steady routines mattered: the bed that held me, the shelf of books, the sill of tiny plastic toys, and the yellow cow that marked morning. Those ordinary things became the frame of my days.

Yet living with my mother was also a constant battle; I learned to walk on eggshells and felt like a prisoner in my own home. Her need for perfection and order pressed on everything; I found solace at my grandparents' house because there I could breathe a little easier. Even there, her strict rules and expectations followed me. Small things set her off: crumbs on the counter, condiments not returned to their designated spot. I tried to be mindful, but no matter how hard I tried, she always found something to criticize. I came to feel that I could never do anything right.

The days she wore dark, dingy T-shirts usually signaled a moody day. On those days I stayed quiet, avoided asking for anything, and tried not to make any mess. It became a constant cycle of fear and anxiety—hoping to avoid her wrath while also feeling invisible and unimportant. On those specific days I wondered if my father ever thought about me or if he even cared. Over time I learned to predict her actions and behaviors and found small, fleeting moments of safety inside those patterns. Still, I never knew what punishment might come if she were upset—another lecture about cleanliness or harsh words that cut into my self-worth. No matter how much I tried to please her, it was never enough. It hurt when she said the house was cleaner when I wasn't there; those words made me feel like a burden. In those moments I wanted to run away or disappear.

STILL, the world outside that apartment was kinder in certain practical ways because of her. She made sure I had the things other kids did: many options in clothes and toys, and papers signed for parent-teacher conferences. She scheduled my doctor visits and let my friends come over without asking if they could stay. Those were the steady gestures she had never been given, and she gave them to me as if to correct an old ledger. The ledger was complicated. Her care arrived as service; her affection was often a practical register rather than a warm hand. That mix left me learning two opposite languages at once: how to tidy to survive, and how to recognize the small, exact ways she loved. I could resent the sharpness and still catalog the kindnesses. Both

CHAPTER THREE

truths sat in me side by side, and both would shape how I sought steadiness later—one by organizing, the other by quietly wanting to be seen.

As an only child, it was easy for me to be spoiled with toys and clothes. But my mother made sure to budget her finances well. When my father started paying child support, she opened a separate savings account just for me, using the money strictly for school supplies, clothes, and necessary appointments. She always made sure to pay the bills first before spending anything extra. I knew this because she would often talk to me about it, and I would see her sitting at the kitchen table budgeting her checkbook.

I remember one day after first or second grade. My mother would always ask me how my day was at the kitchen table. That day, some kids in my class were making fun of another kid for wearing old sneakers. It was a small group I had recently started hanging around with, and I didn't think much of it at the time. But when I told my mother what happened, her tone and expression changed instantly. Her face became stern and stoic as she told me it wasn't right to make fun of other kids for something like that. I felt a jolt run through me. As I tried to defend myself, my words sounded feeble and hollow. Guilt seeped in as she spoke, her voice heavy with disappointment. *"It doesn't matter who started it,"* she said sternly. *"You shouldn't make fun of someone for anything, including what they're wearing. You have no idea what their situation at home is. Not all parents can afford to buy their kids new clothes every year like you get to."*

Her words hit me like a sharp slap, shattering any excuses I'd thought of. She reminded me that she had experienced poverty and not having enough clothes; her family had seven children. That's why she started working at thirteen, just to buy herself basic clothes and shoes. A pang of shame tightened in my chest as she continued, telling me how she was often teased and mocked for not having the latest clothes. The memory of the classroom came back—the kids laughing, the boy with the worn shoes looking down, not fighting back. My mother's lecture washed over me with a new clarity and remorse. I realized how much I had observed without really seeing, how easily I had joined in to fit in. In that moment I promised myself I would never make fun of anyone again. It was a small vow, born at the kitchen table, but it felt like the cleanest thing I had done all day.

CHAPTER FOUR

REKINDLING DISTANT BONDS

My father's visits were random and took me by surprise. On summer days the front door stayed open; the TV filled the living room while my grandmother got dinner ready. He hardly made a sound when he arrived. He never came inside; he preferred the white chairs by the railing while my grandfather stepped out for the adult talk—work, bills, the small measured updates I didn't understand.

The house was a duplex with an open porch, a welcome that was for grown people only. I hugged him when he crouched down to give me a tight hug, and then he'd ask how I was. I never knew what to say; my grandfather's steady answers—"She's doing fine in school, playing like any other child"—closed the conversation for me.

Most visits felt the same, but one stands out; I learned to read the gaps between his coming and going, and that day closed one of those gaps. During the summer months my father and I spent afternoons on the front porch. I played with whatever toys I had or jumped around until he noticed; inside, I was always hoping he was watching. Most of the time he was—his gaze fixed on me even as he talked to my grandfather—sometimes he'd call me over, crouch down and hug me. The hugs felt good, but I wanted more: for him to know me, to choose me. Rarely he'd bring a bag of peanuts and stay longer. Those days felt like being a family, if only briefly. When he left I felt split—glad to have seen him and disappointed that it wasn't longer. I learned to keep my face small and steady so I wouldn't look too eager and risk being hurt. Under that stoicism lived the quieter belief that maybe he didn't care; maybe I was only "a girl," not enough to deserve more time. I watched him walk to his car and wondered, always, if he was going back to his other family—the stepmother and kids my age. I never asked. I waved.

I WAS seven and playing in the front yard when my father's red truck pulled up across the street one day. He climbed out slowly, a heaviness in his shoulders; his face was full of sadness, and he took deep breaths as if gathering strength. Our usual hug that day felt tense and forced; my grandfather's chatter fell flat. Then my father surprised me by standing up to my grandfather and asking for time alone with me. My heart raced; I wanted to help him but didn't know how. When my grandfather walked inside my father looked at me—love and sadness both there. Part of me wanted to ask what was wrong; part of me was afraid of the answer. He breathed, and then said, "*te quiero mucho siempre y quisiera que estuvieras conmigo.*"

[Translation: I love you always and I wish you could be with me.]

His voice cracked. My chest ached: he wanted me and

CHAPTER FOUR

couldn't have me with him. He wiped his eyes, my grandfather returned, and the visit went on as if nothing had happened. Everything had, in fact, changed. I felt guilty for my earlier anger and raw with the old ache of abandonment. I learned then to wrap my feelings in anger as a shield; the loneliness underneath did not go away.

I learned to hide the truth—give short answers that stopped the questions and swallow whatever hurt. I made up small stories to steady myself: that he lived far away, that he was traveling, that someday he would come back and everything would be simple. Distracting myself was easier than letting the absence in; still, holidays like Father's Day tore the cover away and left me raw. Shame rose whenever people asked about my parents. How could I tell them my father didn't care, that he was too busy with his new family to even notice I existed? It hurt to imagine the step-siblings who had the childhood I'd been denied—playing with their dad, going on outings—while I stood outside the life I should have had. Part of me wanted those things so badly I could taste them, but I couldn't say so to my mother. Her steady remarks of him and the barbed comments about his family never felt like jealousy; they were warnings meant to keep me away. I suspected she fed the fear because it was safer for both of us, and I feared betraying her if I admitted I wanted to be near him anyway. Avoiding the truth became second nature; I could not bear that he lived in the same city yet chose to stay away. Sometimes, out of hurt, I lied and said he was dead just to end the questions. Still, under all the stories, anger and a hollow ache rose whenever I let myself think of his absence. I sat on the porch steps until the streetlight blurred, and then I went inside and shut the door.

CHAPTER FIVE

SILENT ECHOES OF A FATHER'S ABSENCE

There were periods in my life when communication with my father was non-existent. By the time I was 12 years old, my visits with my grandparents on weekends and school breaks became less frequent. I felt a sense of isolation and exclusion when my father would mention going on vacations or doing things with his family without me. He didn't realize how much these moments hurt me emotionally. I internalized my feelings and kept them hidden, afraid to express myself and risk rejection from him. Though he occasionally invited me to join in on their activities, I was too scared to go. I was caught between wanting to please my mother by not spending time with my father, and the fear of being around unfamiliar faces. Even when it was just the two of us, our visits were short, usually just grabbing a quick meal and taking a brief stroll in the park since he preferred to avoid crowds. But as I tried to connect with him more, I found myself overwhelmed by confusing and uncomfortable emotions that I couldn't make sense of. It became easier for me to push him away and create excuses for not talking to him than facing

CHAPTER FIVE

those intense feelings. Each visit left me needing time alone in my room to process everything. Yet when I returned home, my mother would bombard me with questions about how it went, what we did, and where we went. Her constant prying and critical comments only added to my overwhelm. This also fueled my decision to distance myself from my father - it seemed like the best option for maintaining some peace in my mind.

AT HOME, things seemed to be going well enough and soon that would change drastically. My mother, a constant source of strength and energy, suddenly found herself injured and unable to work. It was a shock for both of us. For years, I had watched her juggle multiple jobs while still taking care of our household and finances. She was a superhero in my eyes. And now, she was bedridden and dependent on me or her boyfriend for basic tasks. My mother had hurt her back at work that led to back surgery. I couldn't help but feel anger towards her for getting hurt and disrupting our lives. *"Why hadn't she been more careful"*, I thought to myself. But at the same time, guilt gnawed at me as I saw her struggle with pain and frustration every day. It was a conflicting mix of emotions that I didn't know how to handle. And as much as I resented the changes in my life, I also felt a strong empathy for my mother's suffering. It was difficult to reconcile these conflicting feelings towards someone who had always been my support. I wanted to be angry at the situation, angry at the pain that had turned her into a shadow of the strong and mobile woman I once knew. Yet, I couldn't ignore the reality of her struggles, which weighed heavily on my heart.

After my mother's surgery and the long recovery that

followed, she was unable to work for several years. I watched her struggle with pain and rely heavily on medications just to manage her daily life. During her morning and evening medication check-ins, I noticed a resemblance between my mother and my grandmother. As a child, I remembered my grandmother taking an overwhelming amount of pills, and that memory always unsettled me.

In an attempt to find some stability, my mother filed a workman's comp lawsuit, hoping to receive compensation for her situation. But the process was slow and frustrating, and I could see how it affected her mood and spirit. I wanted to support her, but I also worried about what her ongoing struggles meant for our future. However, as the only source of income in our household, her boyfriend wasn't making much, and the financial struggle slowly became a weight on our shoulders. My mother resorted to putting all expenses on credit cards, unknowingly racking up debt. It wasn't until later that we realized the lawsuit would take years before any settlement would come.

THE STRUGGLES CONTINUED to pile on as I entered high school at 15 years old. My mother's back pain and restrictions from doctors still prevented her from working. We lost one of our cars due to missed payments and soon my mother had to file for bankruptcy. With no money and three dogs in tow, our options for finding a new place to live were slim. Luckily, one of my mother's cousins whom we often visited in a small town east from us, had a friend who offered their home to us temporarily. That night, I remember my mother discussing the proposal with her boyfriend and me. It was the beginning of what felt like an

CHAPTER FIVE

endless cycle of packing our bags and constantly moving from place to place.

I remember sitting at the kitchen table with my mother, discussing the possibility of renting a storage room to store our belongings. We had moved to this new place with just a few clothes and necessities, hoping it would be temporary.

THE FAMILY we were staying with seemed nice enough at first - a couple with two teenage children, one my age and the other two years younger. My mother and I shared a bedroom with the daughter, where there were two full-sized beds facing each other and a small TV in between the two beds. But as time passed, things started to change. The lady of the house became distant and we could feel her negative energy towards us. Conversations became non-existent and they stopped inviting us to join them for meals. We tried to be respectful of their space and show our gratitude, but it was clear that something had shifted. It was an uncomfortable feeling, not feeling welcome or wanted in someone else's home. Some days, my mother and I would even go without eating because we didn't want to impose on them anymore. It was a constant struggle between trying to keep the peace and feeling like we were intruders in their home.

The walls felt like they were closing in on us, and we knew we needed to escape as soon as possible. Through an online friend that my mother had met in an AOL chat room during our time living in the cramped apartments, she shared the terrifying experience of being trapped in our current home. Her friend from New York, invited us to stay with him while we got back on our feet.

"*Should we go?*" my mother asked me, her eyes filled with desperation.

"*I don't know,*" I replied.

"*It's pretty far and we don't know anyone there. Do you really want to live in New York?*"

I felt hopeless. There was nothing I could do to change our situation. Being stuck in this strange family's home made me feel like an outsider in a foreign land, trying to navigate life on a never-ending flight. No matter how hard I tried, I couldn't relax. Napping was out of the question because I was constantly on edge, afraid that something might happen. Every move I made was calculated and planned, not only as a good daughter but also as a respectful stranger invading someone else's space. Having any sort of needs or wants seemed like a luxury that we simply couldn't afford.

When my mother presented this new offer to her boyfriend and me, it wasn't an easy decision to make. We were all desperate and had no solid plan or goal for the future. But we knew we had to take a chance and give it a shot. As much as I wanted to escape our current situation, the thought of moving to New York and living with yet another stranger filled me with fear and anxiety. Another move meant more uncertainty and unexpected challenges waiting for us at every turn. But we had no other options, so we packed our bags and prepared for another journey into the unknown.

We crammed our essential items into the trunk of our Chevy Impala, including our three dogs - a large Mastiff taking up the backseat where I was squeezed into a corner. My feet rested on top of bags, maximizing every inch of space in the car. With my mother and her boyfriend taking turns driving, we embarked on a grueling 16-17 hour journey that would take us outside of Syra-

CHAPTER FIVE

cuse, New York. As we drove on, the discomfort only grew - from the cramped quarters to the long drive ahead. And as we passed through Syracuse, I began to feel uneasy. The directions continued to tell us we had more miles to go, and soon enough we found ourselves in a rural countryside far from the city lights. We made a stop at a Walmart along the way, and I remember feeling out of place among all the unfamiliar faces. Coming from diverse Northern Illinois, this area of New York felt like a completely different world. As someone who is brown-skinned, I couldn't help but feel unsafe and out of place compared to what I was used to back home.

When we finally arrived at our destination - a house owned by a man we met through connections - he welcomed us warmly and introduced us to his own pack of dogs. As we settled in for what we thought would be just a few weeks' stay, the man told us about his frequent weekend scavenger hikes with his dogs and encouraged us to make ourselves at home during his absence. But as the evening wore on, I couldn't shake off my unease and confided in my mother that I wanted to go back home - even though we didn't really have one anymore after leaving Rockford. I felt uncomfortable and unsafe in this foreign town, and couldn't imagine trying to attend school here. So the next morning, my mother wrote a letter thanking the man for his hospitality and assistance, but explaining that we didn't feel it was best for us to stay. And with that, we packed up our car once again and left, not looking back as we drove away from the unfamiliar and unwelcome territory.

As we made our way back to Rockford, my mother was on the phone with my uncle Victor, who was currently living with my grandparents. She pleaded for us to stay with them for a little while, and I couldn't help but feel relieved at the thought of finally having a stable place to call home again. Living out of suitcases had become all too familiar, and I couldn't shake off the nagging feeling that maybe we should have just gone with the family in the first place. But deep down, I knew why we hadn't. My mother never quite fit in or received support from her own family. It was this struggle that shaped her into an independent person, always teaching me to figure things out on my own.

When we arrived at my grandparents' house, we dropped off our belongings and immediately headed to our storage unit to retrieve some items that would make our stay more comfortable. My grandparents had moved around town quite a few times since I had been much younger. Their home had a decent-sized finished basement, where we quickly set up our makeshift living space. It may not have been much, but it was home and for that, I felt immensely grateful and relieved. We ended up staying with the family for a couple of months, during which I enrolled back in school as a sophomore. Having missed several weeks due to our frequent moves, this was now my third semester at my third school. I struggled to catch up academically, but being back home with family made it easier to cope.

However, as is often the case in tumultuous circumstances, things didn't remain harmonious for long. At some point, my mother got into a minor disagreement with the family and we decided it was best to leave and find our own space. With limited resources, we moved into a hotel - anything to escape the constant presence of strangers and finally have some breathing room.

CHAPTER FIVE

LIVING in a hotel was the only option we had, but it was far from easy. My mother's boyfriend's job barely covered the cost of our room at Red Roof Inn, and when we moved to Motel 6, we were still cramped in one room with just two full size beds. Going to school provided some relief from our unstable living situation, but it also meant leaving my friends behind and returning to the harsh reality of our situation every afternoon. I couldn't bring myself to share my anxieties with anyone, not even my mother who was living through it all with me. It felt pointless to talk about something we had no control over, and I didn't want anyone to see me as weak or pitiful. The lack of space in our room made it impossible for privacy, and I often drowned out the noise with music on my headphones. Reading was difficult with the constant blaring of the TV. And as for food, we survived on what little we could afford from nearby fast food joints or microwavable meals that we heated up in our room. It was a constant struggle just to get by, and I couldn't help but feel ashamed of our situation and resentful towards those who lived comfortably in their own homes.

After living in a cramped hotel room for several months, my mother eagerly awaited the settlement check that she had been fighting for. She was determined to use the money to purchase a new home and pay off some of our debts. Once the check arrived, we wasted no time in finding and buying our first home.

As first-time homeowners, my mother added her boyfriend's name to the mortgage since he was the sole breadwinner in our household. To celebrate our new life, my mother also splurged on a second vehicle. The shiny Impala quickly became my trusted companion for daily commutes.

Despite having filed for bankruptcy, my mother was able to decorate our new home with some furniture. As we settled into our new surroundings, I couldn't help but feel an overwhelming sense of joy and relief. Finally, we had a place of our own - a sanctuary where we could find peace and stability after years of uncertainty and transience. This was more than just a new house; it was a symbol of hope, security, and normalcy in our lives.

As I stood in my new room, a wave of realization washed over me: the struggles we had faced had taught me more than I ever expected. I had learned to appreciate the small things—a warm meal, a quiet moment, and the feeling of stability that had once seemed so elusive. Each challenge had shaped me, carving a deeper understanding of resilience within my heart.

CHAPTER SIX

HIDDEN STRUGGLES OF SENIOR YEAR

My senior year was the most relaxed and carefree time of my high school experience. Most of my friends had already graduated, leaving me with only two close companions. From the outside, everything seemed fine, but beneath the surface, things were far from okay. We still struggled financially after purchasing our house and car and trying to pay off lingering debts. The initial influx of money seemed to vanish quickly, leaving us in a constant state of financial uncertainty. My mother's back injury had made it impossible for her to work traditional jobs, so she began sporadically working as a cosmetologist —a license she had obtained when I was just five years old to help make ends meet. Slowly, our financial situation worsened again; we faced the threat of foreclosure, lost both cars, and struggled to pay the bills.

As I grew older, my relationship with my mother underwent significant changes. Resentment and anger built up over the years, manifesting in passive-aggressive behavior towards her. Her experiences with back surgery, the ongoing financial struggles, the instability of our living situation, and her toxic relationship with her boyfriend all played a role in shaping her and shifting our once close-knit mother-daughter bond. Looking back, I can't pinpoint a specific event or trigger that caused this change in our relationship. All I know is that I was overwhelmed by a whirlwind of emotions and had no idea how to cope with them. Throughout it all, I never truly felt seen or valued by my mother. I carried a heavy weight of suppressed feelings, often going through the motions of life while feeling isolated and alone, unable to find anyone who could truly understand me.

MEANWHILE, my relationship with my father was strained at best. With each move we made, it became increasingly difficult to maintain any sort of consistent communication or contact with him. Despite my anger towards him, I couldn't deny that he had been there for me in some ways. However, the fact that he didn't seem to care about what my mother and I were going through only deepened the chasm between us. He was aware of our struggles, yet he refused to help, burdened by his own grudges. It wasn't until a year after we moved into our new home that he did something for me—he bought me a car. But even then, the gesture felt superficial, a mere band-aid compared to the deeper issues we faced. As I approached the end of high school and the precipice of adulthood, fear and uncertainty loomed over me like a storm cloud. My life had been turned upside down for years, and now, suddenly, I was expected to step into a "normal" future. But what did normal even mean anymore?

One day, as I watched my mother prepare for a routine doctor's appointment, an overwhelming weight pressed down on

CHAPTER SIX

me. It was a moment of intense despair, one I had felt before, but this time it came with a stronger urge to just end it all. The past few years had felt like a lifetime, and now, facing graduation and the uncertain future ahead, I couldn't bring myself to look forward with the hope or excitement that everyone around me seemed to possess.

As I stood in my room, getting ready for another day of pretending to be okay, the weight of it all crashed down on me. Most of the time, I walked around with a sense of emptiness, like a heavy cloud following me. There were fleeting moments when the cloud would lift—nights spent dancing with friends at quinceaneras—but the exhaustion of faking happiness and hiding my pain was becoming unbearable. Then, as if sensing my breaking point, my mother left the house to get some lab work done, and I watched her through the window as she climbed into the car and drove away. In that moment, a chilling thought struck me: what if this was the last time I would ever see her? I turned away from the window, looking out at the trees and birds outside, trying to find solace in nature, but it wasn't enough. Without a second thought, I raced to the bathroom and grabbed a brand-new bottle of Ibuprofen from the medicine cabinet. The desperate urge to silence the overwhelming pain and anxiety consumed me. In the kitchen, I frantically searched for water and began popping pills into my mouth. My hands trembled with adrenaline as I struggled to swallow them one by one. My mind flashed to all the telenovelas I had watched, where characters effortlessly gulped down handfuls of pills without a second thought or consequence. But here I was, grappling with the reality of my situation, struggling to get even a few down. Frustration and disgust washed over me as I realized that this wasn't going to work like in the telenovelas. Yet something inside me urged me to keep going, to keep drinking until something happened. Panic set in as common sense screamed that this couldn't end well. I needed help. With trembling fingers, I dialed 911, trying to explain through slurred words that I had taken a lot of pills in an attempt to end my life but nothing was happening. As I waited for help to arrive, my vision began to blur, and my movements slowed, as if I were wading through water.

Finally, after what felt like hours but was only a few minutes, the ambulance arrived. My mother had returned home and stood at the doorway, shock and worry etched on her face. I tried to speak, but my tongue felt heavy and uncooperative. The two paramedics walked briskly beside me, gently guiding me into the back of the ambulance. My body felt leaden, and my vision was deteriorating. I closed my eyes, feeling as if I were floating above my own body. The paramedics continued to work, checking my vitals and speaking to me in soothing tones, "*Stay with us, Vanessa; we are almost there.*" As we arrived at the emergency room, I was transferred to a wheelchair and wheeled inside. My consciousness wavered and then faded completely as soon as I sat down. The next thing I remember is waking up in a hospital bed, my mother and high school boyfriend sitting at its foot. They had been anxiously waiting for me to regain consciousness so they could pump my stomach. After a fleeting moment of confusion, a nurse brought in a cup filled with a thick black liquid that smelled strongly of chemicals. I couldn't help but cringe at the sight and odor. "*Is this supposed to make me feel better?*" I asked, hesitantly taking a sip. The nurses nodded, explaining that it was necessary to remove any remaining pills from my system that could cause long-term damage. They added some water and handed me a small can of Sprite to help wash it down. Every sip was a struggle as I fought against the gag reflex threatening to overtake me. The nurses urged me to drink it quickly, but it felt impossible. *"I don't think I can finish all of this,"* I said, pushing the cup away after only managing to drink about half. But before I could protest further, the nausea hit me full force, and I began vomiting violently. It felt like an eternity before I finally stopped retching and felt somewhat stable again. The nurses helped me into a hospital room, where they explained that I would have to stay overnight for observation since I was a patient who had attempted suicide. Due to the seriousness of my condition, they assigned a guard to watch over me 24/7 and removed any potential harmful objects from my room.

My mother had also taken my phone and called my stepsister to inform my father. I remember feeling a mix of emotions when my father arrived at the hospital with my stepmother, only to find my mother in the room as well. There was an awkward silence before anyone spoke. I can still vividly recall that day, both of them asking me separately, *"Why did you do it?"* The weight of their question and the disappointment in their eyes made me want to shrink into myself and disappear. At that moment, I couldn't begin to express the turmoil brewing inside me. It felt like no one truly cared or understood what I was going through. Yet, a part of me secretly hoped someone would reach out, hold me, and tell me that they loved me and that everything would be okay. Deep down, I knew that was just wishful thinking. Growing up, I had never been someone who sought attention or caused trouble for its own sake. But as I sat there in front of my parents, I couldn't help but wonder if creating chaos would finally make them see me and show some concern. However, the thought of further disconnecting from my mother only added to the pain that was already consuming me. My absent father was not someone I could turn to for support, and the rest of my family remained completely oblivious to my struggles. Being around them gave me a sense of belonging, but it was always surface-level. On that day, seeing both my parents show up for me individually made me feel something I had never felt before—truly seen and cared for. Yet, amidst all these conflicting emotions, I couldn't shake the feeling of being alone and unimportant in my own family.

Surrounded by their warm embraces and soothing words, I couldn't help but feel cared for in that moment. And yet, even as I reveled in the attention and comfort, a small voice inside reminded me of the painful journey it took to get here. The struggle and sacrifices that had to be made for me to finally receive what I so desperately needed and wanted. But even as I marveled at this realization, a part of me knew that this fleeting moment would not change everything. It was a brief respite from the turmoil, one that I never expected to happen but was grateful for nonetheless. In that moment, with both of them focused on me, I felt like the center of their world - A rare and precious feeling that I wanted to hold onto forever. But as time passed and I was released from their embrace, not much changed in my life. The only difference was that this traumatic experience served as a reminder to never consider suicide again. It took me some time to fully recover from the emotional toll it had taken on me, but eventually, I found my way back to a place of peace and stability once more.

CHAPTER SEVEN

FROM SHADOWS TO STRENGTH

During my senior year, I took up a part-time job at a department store in the mall to make some extra cash. However, everything changed when I attempted suicide, forcing me to take time off from school and work to recover. The experience left me mentally, emotionally, and physically drained. My body craved extra sleep, as if it instinctively knew it needed time to heal. Even when I was awake, I felt an overwhelming sense of exhaustion and fatigue that went beyond mere lack of sleep. It was a deep weariness that seemed to seep into my bones. For weeks afterward, I struggled with nausea and dizziness, unable to handle much stimulation or sensory overload. As time passed, I began to worry that these feelings would never go away, that this was going to be my new normal. But eventually, after a month of rest and recovery, I finally started to feel like myself again.

That summer, at the age of 19, I decided it was time to find a new job. That's when I got hired at Hooters. However, it quickly became a short-lived experience for me. I soon realized that this environment wasn't a good fit. Flirting felt almost like a requirement to earn tips, and that just wasn't who I was. At that time, I was shy and closed off, not one to easily trust others. I spent most of my shifts in the kitchen area washing dishes when it wasn't very busy. The job made me uncomfortable, and it was one of the first times I encountered racist comments from customers. Feeling increasingly out of place, I ultimately decided to leave.

MY MOTHER'S unhealthy relationship with her boyfriend had reached a boiling point, and I could feel the tension rising. There was constant arguing and he would disappear for days at a time, until my mother couldn't take it anymore and kicked him out for good. But even then, things didn't get any better. My mother was struggling emotionally and I felt like it was my responsibility to fix it. She never expressed her true feelings, so I was left trying to decipher her moods and make sure she was okay. Our relationship had shifted from mother-daughter to almost friends or co-dependents. As I entered my teenage years, I saw my mother lean on me more and more for support. She didn't have any other close relationships or friends to turn to. But as she changed into someone I barely recognized, I started to lose the strong, authoritative figure who used to rule our household. And as much as I tried to support and help her, there were moments where I felt like the roles had switched and she was relying on me too much.

I love my mother and wanted to help her, but at the same time, I resented feeling like I had to take care of her instead of focusing on my own life. It was a constant internal struggle

CHAPTER SEVEN

between wanting to be there for her and wanting to break free from this chaotic cycle we were stuck in.

The aftermath of my mother's boyfriend leaving was devastating yet freeing. Our already tight finances became even more strained, and it seemed like there was no escape from the constant struggle to keep a roof over our heads and food on the table. The stress was suffocating, and I did everything in my power to avoid facing it head on. But it always found its way back to us, never fully going away before rearing its ugly head again.

When he left, he disappeared without a trace, as if he had been swallowed whole by the earth. And with his departure came a renewed financial struggle. We resorted to scrimping and saving every penny just to afford groceries, often feeling embarrassed as we walked through the store with a fear of going over our budget and having to put items back.

Amidst all of this chaos, I was also trying to attend community college. But with each passing semester, my grades began to slip as it became increasingly difficult to focus and stay motivated. Eventually, after my third semester, I had no choice but to drop out, a decision that weighed heavily on me. I had no one to confide in about my disappointment and feelings of failure. When my mother tried to offer words of encouragement, I couldn't help but feel a tinge of resentment towards her for not being the stable and mature figure I needed during such a crucial time. College itself felt like an insurmountable challenge at times, as I constantly doubted my intelligence and struggled to concentrate. It was nothing like high school, where I excelled. I had dreams of making my family proud by being the first to graduate from college, but those hopes were shattered. Yet, amidst all of this disappointment, I couldn't properly grieve because our immediate survival took precedence over any personal aspirations or accomplishments.

AS WE FELL BEHIND on our payments, the looming threat of foreclosure hung over us. Panic and fear consumed us as we realized we had no idea how to seek help or if it even existed for first time homeowners like us. Soon enough, we lost our house. And just when I thought things couldn't get any worse, my trusty white Pontiac Bonneville, the car my father had gifted, had began to have major mechanical issues. The cost of repairs outweighed the value of the car itself, leaving me with no transportation and no way to get another vehicle. My father was the only person who could possibly help me, but he wasn't being very cooperative. I reluctantly confided in him about our situation, and he suggested I move in with him. It wasn't the first time he had offered this solution. While I appreciated his offer, I couldn't take it. In choosing to live with my father, I couldn't help but feel like I was betraying my mother. It also meant taking on the weight of responsibility for her safety and well-being. If I left her behind in her worst time, would I ever be able to contact her again? I feared my father's control over me, knowing he could use his financial support to dictate where I went and what I did. Yet, the thought of continuing to struggle and burden my mother weighed heavily on my conscience. She had already been through so much in her life and it didn't seem fair that I got to escape it all just because I wanted an easier life. My father often made comments insinuating that my mother was unstable and couldn't properly care for me due to her choices and actions. At the time, I vehemently disagreed, knowing there were nuances

CHAPTER SEVEN

and details he was unaware of. But as an adult, I can see where he was coming from. In this situation, everything felt out of control and no matter what decision I made, someone would end up hurt.

We had no car, no money, and no one to turn to for help. That's when my grandparents stepped in. We managed to borrow someone's truck and were able to rent a smaller storage unit for our furniture. My grandparents had yet moved into another duplex apartment that they owned, with some of my uncles living upstairs as bachelors while my grandparents resided downstairs. They gave me a bedroom next to theirs where I finally had a space of my own, while my mother stayed in the basement that they had converted into a makeshift living area for her. Despite the circumstances, my mother tried to make it feel like home by decorating with some of our belongings from the old house. My mother continued to work part-time at the hair salon with rides from my grandfather, while I stayed home with my grandparents without means of transportation. It was during one of these moments in the backyard, walking our poor dogs who had stuck by us through it all, that I couldn't help but wonder: "*What is life?*". As I watched them sniff and explore the small yard on leashes, memories flooded back of our previous struggles and sacrifices. "*Here we go again,*" I thought to myself, not expecting to find ourselves in this situation once more.

We lived with my grandparents for several months, a temporary arrangement that was soon disrupted by a confrontation between them and my mother. The details of the argument have faded from my memory, but I remember the urgency in my mother's voice as she insisted we needed to leave.

She worked at a local salon where a new employee had recently been hired, a woman slightly younger than my mother with two children - an eight-year-old daughter and a toddler son. This woman had a record, filled with petty crimes like theft and identity fraud, as well as a past of drug use. Despite her history, my mother became friends with this woman. She often gave people the benefit of the doubt, but even I could sense something off about her. There was a palpable negative energy surrounding her. I couldn't quite put my finger on it, but I knew to keep my distance. One evening, while we were in the basement of our temporary home, my mother shared an offer this woman had mentioned. She had extra space and offered for us to stay with her. I would be paid to watch her young son while they worked, and we could use the basement to store any belongings instead of paying for a storage unit. My entire body tensed up at the mention of this offer. "*No*," I blurted out before my mother could even respond. My anger boiled as I watched my mother dismiss my concerns and insist on staying with this sketchy woman. The tension between us grew as we shared a bedroom, our belongings scattered throughout the basement she had offered to store them in. I could sense something off about this woman, her past sob story just another tool in her manipulative arsenal. She didn't have much but was all too willing to use people like my mother, who couldn't resist helping those in need. And now she was suggesting we let her borrow our furniture? My blood boiled at the thought of this woman taking advantage of our kindness, using it for her own gain. But my mother seemed blinded by empathy, unable to see the danger lurking beneath this woman's facade of neediness. It all came crashing down when she offered to sign me up for a paid program to watch her infant son. I knew deep down it was just another ploy to control and exploit us. But how could I refuse when my own mother was so eager to please? Our fear and uncertainty only intensified as we settled into this

CHAPTER SEVEN

temporary home, unsure of what manipulative schemes this woman had up her sleeve next.

Weeks passed with an ever-present sense of danger lurking in the house. My mother and the lady would go to work, leaving me alone with the baby. But I never felt safe or comfortable, a constant unease gnawing at my gut.

One weekend, my aunt offered to take us on errands and my mother informed the lady of our plans. We left early in the morning, around 9 or 10 am, promising to return in a couple of hours. But when we opened the front door upon returning, we were met with utter shock and disbelief. The entire house was empty, stripped bare of all our belongings. I stood there, frozen and speechless for what felt like an eternity, while rage burned inside me. My mother's expression mirrored mine as she likely exclaimed "*what the fuck*" in disbelief. The anger and fear consumed me as I screamed at her, blaming her for not listening to my warnings about the lady's past criminal activity. Our furniture may not have been expensive or valuable, but each piece held sentimental value and represented hard-earned money. How could someone be so heartless as to take everything from us without a second thought? I cursed God for allowing this to happen, questioning why we were targeted by such a ruthless thief. Was it to sell our belongings for quick cash? We were left dumbfounded by the sudden disappearance of everything we owned and feared what would happen next. This person had no regard for kindness or mercy, only their own selfish desires driving them to commit such an unspeakable act against us. My mother seemed unfazed, but I was filled with rage and disbelief. How could this woman have planned this out without us suspecting anything? And where was God in all of this? I felt abandoned and alone, my anger towards Him growing more intense by the minute. My mother's calmness only added fuel to my already burning fire.

"*How are you not angry?*" I shouted at her, unable to contain my emotions.

"*Yes, I am angry,*" she responded calmly.

"*But those were just material things and what's done is done.*"

Frustrated and confused, my mother picked up the phone and called her work, hoping someone had seen or heard from the woman who had robbed us. But she was a no-show, vanished without a trace. With no leads, no money, and no car, the truth settled over us like a weight we couldn't push off—we were officially homeless.

Just when despair threatened to swallow us, the salon manager made a call of her own. She knew someone who might be able to help. Minutes later, he pulled up in an old red Corvette, sunglasses hiding his eyes. After hearing our story from the manager, he didn't hesitate. He offered his help without conditions, without even knowing us.

On the ride back to his house, he gave us pieces of his story. He lived with his son, who was recovering from a serious car accident that had left him bound to a cast and unable to get around on his own. His son's girlfriend and their young toddler were also staying there, filling the house with the kind of noise and chaos that comes with small children. Space was already tight, but he assured us there was still an extra bedroom for us.

I didn't know what to make of it. We were strangers, and yet here he was, opening his door as if it were the most natural thing in the world. His generosity startled me—an unearned kindness at a moment when we had nothing to give in return.

We gathered the few belongings we had left and piled into

CHAPTER SEVEN

his car. My mother, always quick to show gratitude, thanked him over and over, apologizing that we had nothing to offer in return. He brushed it off with a wave of his hand, as if her words were unnecessary, then steered us across town. By some stroke of fortune, his house was not far from the salon where she worked.

It was clear, even then, that this man had known hardship himself. His life bore the weight of struggle, yet still he found it in his heart to extend kindness to strangers. When we arrived, he led us inside, pointing out the bedroom we could use before introducing us to the rest of his family. Later that day, as my mother sat at the table with him, her voice soft with curiosity as they began to share their stories, I felt like an intruder in someone else's world. Everything was unfamiliar—the cadence of their voices, the smell of their food, the worn furniture that had shaped years I wasn't part of. And yet, beneath my discomfort, I could sense a current of genuine warmth. These people had opened their home to us without hesitation, and there was no mistaking the kindness behind that gesture.

Still, I couldn't shake the unease of depending on them. Neither he nor his son was working at the time, and I hated the thought of adding to their burden. To avoid overstaying my welcome, I often tagged along with my mother to the salon, even if it meant hours of waiting with nothing to do. At the house, I kept my distance, rarely sitting in the living room where they spent their afternoons watching television.

At the time, I mistook their quietness for indifference. But looking back now, I understand it differently. Their stillness, their willingness to let us come and go without question, was not detachment—it was empathy. They knew what it meant to endure hard seasons, and their way of helping was to offer space, acceptance, and a roof overhead, no matter how little they had themselves.

The family was kind and welcoming, but we didn't stay long. My mother was determined to find a place of our own, no matter how modest, as soon as she could scrape together a few paychecks. Independence, even in its smallest form, meant everything to her by that point.

After a few short weeks of searching, she found it—a rundown house on the West Side of town, not far from where he lived and close to the salon. It sat on the corner of a busy street, the kind of corner where danger never felt far away. The green siding paint that looked dirty and peeling, with an old porch. But it was ours, and that was enough.

When we moved in, the emptiness of the place was almost startling. The rooms echoed with our footsteps, bare walls with no furniture, no decorations, nothing to soften the sharpness of starting over. Most glaring of all was the absence of a refrigerator. My mother pleaded with the landlord, reminding him that even the most basic home needed one. Weeks passed before he finally delivered—an old, dented appliance but at least it kept our food cold. Until then, we survived with coolers, packing and repacking bags of melting ice just to preserve a few groceries. It was far from comfortable, but it was a start.

BY THEN I WAS TWENTY-TWO, and eager to find work and contribute to our new home. With little education and almost no experience, my options were slim. Out of necessity, I turned to a temp agency, which placed me at a pharmaceutical packaging

CHAPTER SEVEN

company as a packer. The work was repetitive and unremarkable, but I showed up every day and did what was asked of me.

After several months, I was occasionally pulled from the line to assist the maintenance group. I didn't think much of it at first, but eventually, they offered me a full-time position as a Maintenance Coordinator. It wasn't the job of my dreams—not even close to anything I had ever imagined for myself—but it came with something I hadn't had in years: stability. A steady paycheck. Health insurance.

The tasks were often mundane, but I carried them out with a quiet pride. Each day I clocked in and out was a reminder that I was no longer drifting, no longer entirely dependent on the kindness of others. It may not have been the life I had envisioned, but it was a beginning—and for the first time in a long time, that was enough.

CHAPTER EIGHT

FINDING BALANCE IN CHAOS

Since graduating high school, life had become a whirlwind—work, bills, responsibilities, and the constant scramble to keep up. In all that busyness, my health slipped quietly into the background. I ate whatever was quick and convenient, rarely moved my body, and hardly noticed until the pounds began to add up. By twenty-five, I was twenty-five pounds heavier.

One morning, as I stood in front of the mirror getting ready, the truth stared back at me. My body had changed. My hand gripped at the skin on my stomach, and before I could stop myself, the words came out in a whisper I'd never say to anyone else: *fat bitch*. Shame pooled in my chest, heavy and suffocating. But this wasn't new. I had been at war with my reflection long before the scale tipped higher.

Growing up, I had always been thin, and instead of praise, I was met with ridicule. Family, classmates—even friends—picked me apart with casual remarks: *you need to eat more, you're too small, do you even eat?* At first, I brushed it off. But

CHAPTER EIGHT

over time, those words burrowed deep, making me question if my body would ever be "enough."

The irony was that I had never struggled with food. I ate regularly, never restricted, and yet the world around me insisted on defining me as lacking. The constant commentary chipped away at my self-worth, carving insecurities where none had existed before.

BY TWENTY-FIVE, the insults had flipped. I wasn't "too small" anymore—I was "too big." And even though I hated what I saw in the mirror, I did nothing to change it. Instead, I carried the weight of those words with me, heavier than any number on the scale.

As the weight crept on, I became skilled at hiding. Baggy clothes, strategic angles, avoiding mirrors—I did whatever I could to conceal the body I no longer recognized. My once slim frame now carried curves I hadn't asked for. My breasts and hips had grown, but so had everything else, and none of it felt like mine. With every extra pound, my energy dipped lower, my confidence eroded, and I knew something had to change.

The thought of stepping foot into a gym terrified me. I had never been athletic, never touched a dumbbell, never moved in that world. Gyms, to me, were places for people who already belonged there. But desperation can push you past fear, and one day I signed a membership at Anytime Fitness.

In the beginning, I was lost. I'd walk in, look around at the machines with no idea where to start, and half the time ended up scrolling on my phone to avoid the awkwardness. My visits were inconsistent, my workouts unfocused. I wanted results but had no real plan.

Eventually, I admitted to myself that winging it wasn't working. Swallowing my pride, I hired a personal trainer for one 45-minute session each week. The workouts were intense—I left drenched in sweat and sore for days—but even after months of showing up, my body barely changed. The scale refused to budge, and my reflection looked the same.

What I didn't realize then was that transformation isn't just built in the gym. I was showing up for workouts, but my diet stayed exactly the same. I wasn't resistant to change—I just didn't know how to change. Six months passed, and though the disappointment weighed on me, a small part of me knew the truth: one session a week, without addressing the rest of my habits, was never going to be enough.

ONE MORNING, as I opened my eyes, the first thing that met me wasn't the light through the blinds—it was the familiar sting of self-criticism. My body felt heavy, foreign. The sight of myself made me want to pull the covers back over my head and disappear.

But then something shifted. It wasn't gentle or gradual—it was sharp, like a snap deep in my chest. A heat rose inside me, a stubborn flame at the base of my spine. For the first time in a long time, I felt anger not just at my reflection, but at the idea of giving up on myself. *Enough,* I thought. Something has to change. The question was—where do I even begin?

The shadow of my family's health struggles loomed large in my mind: diabetes, heart disease, the quiet resignation of bodies

CHAPTER EIGHT

breaking down too soon. I didn't want that to be my future. Yet I was lost when it came to food, to "dieting." I had seen quick fixes, crash diets, and calorie-cutting schemes play out, only to collapse just as quickly as they started. I knew I didn't want that. If I was going to fight for change, it couldn't be temporary—it had to be sustainable. Still, I couldn't let not knowing every step stop me from taking the first one. So I set a promise with myself: imperfect action was better than none at all.

Armed with the little guidance my coach had given me and a willingness to pay closer attention to what I was eating, I stepped forward into the unknown. It wasn't going to be easy—I knew that. But it had to start somewhere. And that morning, with both fear and determination swirling inside me, I decided it would start with me.

During that time, my days and nights blurred together in a cycle of research. I devoured blogs, articles, and books on fitness, scribbling notes in spiral-bound notebooks until the margins were crammed with facts, diagrams, and half-formed insights. Writing everything down helped me not only remember but also process—it gave me a sense of control, a way to connect the dots. Whenever I studied a new topic, I pulled from multiple sources, cross-checking, comparing, and asking myself questions: What's the common thread? Does this resonate with me? Where's the evidence? I trusted not just the data but my intuition, looking for what felt both true and practical. Only after combing through pages of research would I consider applying what I learned to my own life.

This was how my journey into fitness truly began. For months, I toggled back and forth between nutrition and exercise, adjusting my meals while experimenting with different workouts. At first, my only goal was to lose fat, to be thin. But over time, something shifted. My gym visits became more frequent, my sessions more intense, and my mindset evolved. I realized I wasn't chasing skinny—I was chasing strength, sustainability, a way of living I could carry with me long-term.

Like titrating medication, I introduced changes slowly, in doses I could handle. A tweak to a meal here, a new lift there. With patience—and more grace than I was used to giving myself—those bite-sized adjustments became habits. At first, discomfort was easy to ignore; my hunger for change drowned it out. But as weeks turned into months, it became a balancing act, learning to hold discipline and self-compassion in the same hand.

It all blurred together: the note-taking, the meal prep, the sweat-soaked gym sessions. Yet beneath the whirlwind, there was a current pulling me forward. Motivation, determination, and a growing vision of who I might become if I didn't give up.

Through countless hours of research, trial and error, and stubborn persistence, I pushed forward on my weight-loss journey. It was far from glamorous. Many days blurred into a haze of repetition—measuring food, logging workouts, dragging myself to the gym and wondering if any of it would ever pay off. There were moments of doubt so heavy I questioned whether my efforts mattered at all.

But slowly, change came. After a year of steady work, the weight I'd carried melted away. The transformation wasn't fast, and it wasn't flashy, but it was mine. I chose sustainability over shortcuts, habits over hacks. It required sacrifice and patience, but staying put in the same house for two years gave me the stability I needed to finally invest in myself.

Of course, it wasn't smooth sailing. Motivation slipped, especially when my schedule collided with my mother's—we shared a car, and her needs often came first. At one point, I felt myself

CHAPTER EIGHT

sliding backward, terrified that all my progress would unravel. That fear lit something in me, and I made a decision that felt almost unthinkable at the time: I would start working out at 3 a.m., before my shifts at work.

The first mornings were brutal. My alarm sliced through the darkness, my body begging me to stay in bed. But I forced myself up, pulling on gym clothes in silence, brushing my teeth, then heading to the kitchen for fuel—usually a banana or rice cakes with peanut butter, washed down with a protein shake. I had learned quickly that exercising on an empty stomach left me dizzy and weak, so this small ritual became my armor.

Over time, what once felt impossible became routine. The stillness of the gym at that hour grew to feel like a gift. With no crowds or chatter, I could focus, zeroing in on my form, learning to trust my body, and slowly building a quiet confidence I had never known before. After a few months, the 3 a.m. grind wasn't a punishment—it was part of who I was. Showing up for myself had become as natural as brushing my teeth.

AFTER TWO YEARS OF SWEAT, discipline, and sacrifice, I finally let myself stop and take it all in. The pounds were gone—and more importantly, I had kept them off for an entire year. Sometimes it felt unreal, as if I were walking through a dream I didn't want to wake from. I'd stand in front of the mirror, tilting my head, tracing the changes, half-expecting my old reflection to return. More than once I pinched myself, just to be sure it wasn't all in my imagination. What I saw staring back wasn't just a smaller body—it was proof of what I was capable of. For the first time, I truly understood the power of the mind–body connection. The weight I carried had never been just physical; it was the stories I told myself, the doubts I fed, the limits I believed were true. I realized that our greatest barriers often live in our heads, not in our muscles.

Through this process, I learned that personality shapes the journey. Some people need accountability, others thrive on structure, and still others learn best through trial and error. I was a mix of all three. I needed guidance to start, but the real work came in re-evaluating my own lifestyle—carving out time, rewriting routines, and deciding every day to show up for myself. This was more than weight loss. It was proof that I could build discipline, that I could choose a different path than the one I had feared was waiting for me.

> I've come to understand that childhood experiences leave a deeper mark on our bodies than most people realize. Trauma and adversity shape the way we cope, the habits we cling to, and the comfort we seek. For some, the weight of unresolved pain shows up in overeating, in chronic stress, or in the body's quiet rebellion through hormone imbalance. I began to see how cortisol, anxiety, and self-sabotage could all be tied back to wounds we never asked for but still carried. Sometimes, holding on to weight isn't just about food—it's about survival, a shield the body builds to keep us safe.

My confidence grew one small victory at a time. Each meal prepped, each workout finished, each pound kept off became proof that I could trust myself. Slowly, meal prepping became

CHAPTER EIGHT

second nature, a ritual of chopping, portioning, and stacking containers neatly in the fridge. It was my way of taking control, of ensuring consistency. But change doesn't happen in a vacuum.

One evening, I sat across from my mother at the table for what had become a rare shared meal. She looked at me with soft eyes and said how much she missed cooking for both of us, how strange it felt to eat alone so often. Her words caught me off guard, settling heavy in my chest. In all my determination to create new habits, I hadn't stopped to consider what it meant for her—for the small rituals of connection we had unknowingly lost. A pang of guilt ran through me. My pursuit of health had given me strength, but it had also carved quiet distance between us.

As the number on the scale crept closer to my goal, a strange fear began to set in. Reaching the weight was one thing, but maintaining it? That was uncharted territory. I didn't know how many calories my body actually needed or what balance of cardio and strength would keep me steady. The idea that I would have to keep this up forever felt overwhelming, almost suffocating. Hungry for guidance, I turned to the one place that seemed to have all the answers: social media. Instagram quickly became my platform of choice, a curated feed of fitness influencers whose posts kept me motivated and hungry to learn. I followed women who sculpted their bodies into something I had never seen before—muscular yet feminine, powerful yet graceful.

That was when I stumbled upon the world of competition: IFBB and NPC athletes with physiques that looked carved from stone. Not all the women I admired competed, but their discipline and dedication were undeniable. They weren't chasing the fragile thinness of a Victoria's Secret model. By 2015, a shift was happening—women were chasing muscle, tone, and strength. The "skinny" ideal was giving way to something bolder, and for the first time, I saw a vision of what my body could be, not just what I wanted to escape.

When I saw the toned physiques of the women I followed online, something inside me lit up. I had a new goal to chase—the bikini division. The lean, sculpted look of those athletes drew me in, and I began researching every detail of how to achieve it. I studied training splits, meal plans, stage presence, even posing, convinced that if I just followed the blueprint, I could get there too. But even with all the knowledge I was gathering, I was still stumbling. My fear of regaining weight pushed me toward restriction, cutting calories so low that my body had little energy to grow or recover. At the gym, I threw myself into workouts with relentless intensity, especially for my lower body. I wore soreness like a badge of honor, convincing myself that if I couldn't walk properly the next day, it meant I was working hard enough. But deep down, I wondered if this kind of pain was really normal.

Looking back, I see how my determination was actually holding me back. I didn't yet understand that rest was just as vital as training, that muscles don't grow in the gym but in the recovery that follows. I skipped rest days, punished my body with overtraining, and starved it of the nutrients it needed to build. I thought I was accelerating my progress, when in reality I was stalling it.

>It was a painful but necessary lesson: *discipline without balance can become its own form of sabotage.*

CHAPTER EIGHT

My training routine, if I could call it that, was mostly high-volume exercises thrown together without structure or direction. I pushed myself hard but without clarity, chasing fatigue rather than progress. Meanwhile, nutrition felt like a maze with no exit—every article, every influencer, every "plan" contradicted the next. The more I searched for answers, the more overwhelmed I felt. Food itself became the enemy. The macro calculator I stumbled upon suggested I increase my calories, but the thought of eating more made my chest tighten. Anxiety crept in at every meal, and soon every bite felt like a gamble I couldn't afford to lose. Protein, carbs, fat—it didn't matter. I feared them all, convinced that one wrong move would undo everything I had worked for. I didn't have the language for it then, but now I know: it was disordered eating.

Sometimes the mirror betrayed me, showing a body I didn't recognize. My reflection seemed distorted, as if my mind couldn't catch up with the weight I had already lost. It was only when I stepped on the scale that reality would slap me back into place: over twenty pounds gone. Yet my eyes still searched for flaws, my mind still whispered I wasn't enough. The war inside was relentless—carbs versus fats, hunger versus fear. Each meal felt like a battlefield. And I fought it mostly alone. With no one to confide in, I leaned on intuition, trial and error, and sheer persistence. Slowly, painfully, I began exposing myself to the foods I feared, retraining my mind bite by bite.

Over time, I learned how to increase my intake without spiraling into panic, how to hit my macros with a confidence that once felt impossible.

That process taught me something no book or influencer could: *nutrition is as much psychological as it is physical.*

But progress had its limits. My body hit a plateau, aching under the weight of exhaustion. I was stuck. For so long, pride and stubbornness kept me from admitting I needed help. I thought I should be able to figure it out on my own. But the harder I pushed, the clearer it became: I couldn't.

So, with equal parts nerves and hope, I began the search for a coach. My criteria were strict: integrity, authenticity, passion, professionalism. I observed from a distance, watching how different trainers carried themselves, how they treated their clients. Finally, after weeks of scouting, I reached out to a handful of coaches. One stood out—a woman whose energy and presence aligned with everything I was looking for. I signed on to work with her for six months.

For the first time, I wasn't carrying it all alone. During our six months together, my coach started with the basics—where my body was, what my habits looked like, and where I wanted to go. I told her about my desire to build muscle, but also confessed the fear I carried around food, the way increasing calories felt like stepping off a cliff. Instead of dismissing my worries, she listened. As I immersed myself deeper into the fitness community, I began to see a pattern. I wasn't the only one afraid of eating more. Other women were voicing the same struggles, the same tug-of-war between wanting strength and fearing weight gain. That realization brought me comfort I didn't expect. I wasn't broken; I wasn't alone.

But my coach's role stretched beyond macros and training

CHAPTER EIGHT

plans. She became a steady presence, someone I could lean on when doubt crept in. Her encouragement created a sense of safety I hadn't felt in a long time. She didn't just hand me a plan—she reminded me I was capable of following through with it. Her experience as both a lifestyle coach and someone who had worked with athletes gave her a rare perspective. She understood the nuances, the emotional side of the process, not just the science. With every check-in and every conversation, I felt more supported, more seen. For the first time, fitness didn't feel like a lonely battle.

AS 2015 CAME to a close and 2016 began, my path forward felt clear: I was going to become a certified personal trainer. Fitness had reshaped my life, and now I wanted to make it official. I believed a certification would be the key to everything—that it would hand me the secrets I had been chasing for years. My ticket to becoming an expert. If I'm honest, my motivation wasn't entirely selfless. I wanted to help people, yes, but I also feared I wasn't "fit enough" to be taken seriously. Part of me believed that unless I wore the look of a trainer—the lean muscle, the polished physique—no one would listen. So my drive to become certified was just as much about proving myself as it was about guiding others.

I chose the ISSA certification program, paid the fee, and soon a thick textbook landed in my hands. I carried it everywhere—reading during lunch breaks at work, highlighting chapters late into the night, scribbling notes across the margins. But as I worked through the material, reality settled in. There were no secrets hidden in those pages, no shortcuts to mastery. Certification was only a starting point.

I began to understand that what sets a coach apart isn't the letters after their name, but their willingness to keep learning—to blend formal education with personal research, trial and error, and hands-on experience. Every body is different. Every journey requires a unique approach. The truth is, becoming a successful coach isn't about knowing it all. It's about never closing the door on growth. It's about being willing to experiment, to fail, to learn again, even if it means becoming your own guinea pig in the process. That realization shifted something in me. I had once thought certification would make me enough. But what I discovered instead was far more valuable:

---

the humility to keep evolving, and the courage to never stop learning.

CHAPTER NINE

PACKING UP AND MOVING ON

Our time in that house had been steady for four years, but stability has a way of slipping through our fingers. When issues with the landlord surfaced, we were once again faced with the exhausting task of packing up our lives and searching for a new place to land. Finding a home that would accept multiple dogs felt impossible, and time was not on our side.

With my grandmother's passing years earlier, the family dynamic had shifted. My grandfather, now alone, offered us his house once more. But walking through the door, it was clear things were different. The warmth that once lived there—the decorations, the knickknacks, the small touches of her presence—were gone. The house felt colder now, stripped of her energy.

We ended up in the basement, trying to carve out a living space among the remnants of a life that no longer existed. Boxes stacked against the walls. My grandmother's furniture crowding the room. The air itself seemed heavy, darker and gloomier without her. This time, there was no help from family. My uncles refused, and my mother suggested we leave most of our furniture behind. We took only what was necessary, but even that seemed to press in on us once it was crammed into the basement. At night, I shared a bed with my mother in the same room she had once slept in. That closeness made me feel safe, but beneath it was a quiet frustration—an ache that we were here again, struggling, circling the same cycle I longed so desperately to escape.

Living in my grandfather's house, I found myself caught between two worlds—trying to maintain the healthy lifestyle I had fought so hard to build, while also facing the uncertainty of our next move. My mother and I brainstormed constantly, but the reality of our situation weighed on every conversation. With multiple dogs in tow, our options were slim. Each online search ended the same way: houses too expensive, rentals unwilling to accept pets, neighborhoods that felt unsafe.

The thought of buying a house together began to creep into my mind. The idea felt enormous, almost reckless, but I couldn't ignore the truth—my mother couldn't afford a home on her own, and I couldn't stand the thought of us repeating this cycle again and again. The decision pressed heavily on me. I was steady at my job and grateful for the opportunities it provided, but I knew deep down it wasn't my forever path. Still, I had to trust that when the time came, fate would show me where to go.

In the present, I was faced with the choice of what truly mattered: independence, or stepping into the role of co-provider. It was one of the hardest decisions I had ever made, offering to buy a house with my mother. After months of searching and failed attempts, luck finally tipped in our favor. We found a place. Papers were signed, and keys pressed into our hands. On moving day, as I unpacked my belongings, a strange feeling washed over me. The weight of all our past struggles hung in the

CHAPTER NINE

air, but so did something lighter, something unfamiliar: hope. For the first time, I allowed myself to believe that maybe—just maybe—this would be the last time we had to start over from nothing.

BY THE SPRING OF 2017, I found myself pausing to take stock of the ground I had covered. Two mini bulks, countless tweaks to my workouts and nutrition—my body had transformed again and again, reshaped by discipline and experimentation. And now, a new thought was beginning to press against the edges of my mind: competition.

The idea of stepping on a bodybuilding stage both thrilled and terrified me. Competing was expensive, demanding, and not something to take lightly. Before I even considered it, I needed to know—really know—that I could handle the rigor of an intense prep. I wanted to push my limits, to test not just my body but my discipline, to see how far I could go. In my heart, I wasn't chasing a regional trophy or a fleeting title. If I was going to do it, I wanted to aim higher. To dream of becoming a pro athlete. And yet, doubt lingered. Was this truly meant for me, or was it another version of chasing validation?

> Sometimes what we want most isn't what serves us best, and trusting my own desires felt like stepping into fog.

Another force tugging at me was the desire to help others. I knew what it felt like to lose weight, to battle self-doubt, to crawl toward consistency. But if I wanted to guide others, I needed to sharpen my own tools. More experience. More proof. And so, I decided: I would commit to a 14-week cut. Impatience and comparison—so often fueled by endless scrolling on social media—whispered that I wasn't enough yet. In response, I threw myself into the gym every single day, convinced that more effort equaled more progress. Determination carried me, but so did trepidation. Still, by late winter, I was locked in. Fourteen weeks ahead of me, a test not just of body, but of mind.

As the weeks passed, my body began sending warning signals I didn't yet know how to read. My menstrual cycle vanished, leaving me disoriented and oddly disconnected from the very rhythms that once grounded me. A heavy fog settled over my mind, making even simple thoughts feel out of reach. The mirror showed progress, but my body told another story. Clumps of hair came out in my hands, a stark reminder of the nutrients I was denying myself. Despite the summer heat, I shivered constantly, the chill of an extreme caloric deficit seeping into my bones. Irritability became my baseline. My libido disappeared altogether. My energy—once a steady flame—flickered to its lowest point.

And yet, at first, I reveled in what I saw. My reflection revealed an unprecedented level of leanness, cuts and definition I had never thought possible for myself. Pride swelled, ego flared —I had done it. I had pushed my body further than ever before. But hindsight paints a sharper picture. That cut, though "successful" on the surface, was riddled with mistakes. Yes, I had improved upon my first attempt at dieting—more knowledge, more structure—but I was still miles away from balance. The process had cost me more than I realized at the time. And while

CHAPTER NINE

it left me lean, it also left me depleted. It was a lesson written in hunger, exhaustion, and fragile hair strands:

Progress without wisdom is just another form of self-destruction.

Even with my body sending every warning signal it could, I clung to my physique as long as I could. For three more months, I pushed through the summer on low calories and relentless cardio, determined to hold onto the leanness I had worked so hard to achieve. But eventually, the cracks became too wide to ignore. My body was exhausted, my mind unraveling. That was when I came face to face with something I had only ever heard whispered about in the fitness community: body dysmorphia. At first, it was subtle—a glance in the mirror where I felt a pang of doubt, a small insecurity brushed off as normal. But before long, it consumed me. My thoughts became a constant loop of comparison—measured against the flawless physiques I scrolled past on Instagram, against my own reflection from weeks earlier, against an ever-shifting standard I could never quite reach. The fear of gaining weight stalked me everywhere, even into the clothes I wore. I began to worry that I wasn't just unhealthy beneath the surface—I worried that I wasn't enough.

Looking back now, it's difficult to capture the full weight of that struggle, how loud the self-criticism grew, how small I felt inside my own skin. But the lesson it left behind is clear:

> physical transformation means nothing if it comes at the expense of mental health. The pursuit of fitness is never just about the body—it's about the mind that has to live in it.

I wrestled with my self-image in the shadows of my own mind, locked in a tug-of-war I couldn't seem to win. Even with more lean mass than body fat, I refused to admit what was becoming clear—that my relationship with food and my body carried anorexic tendencies. I brushed it off, telling myself I was fine, that this was just discipline. But deep down, my intuition kept whispering otherwise. That inner voice—the same gut instinct that had guided me since childhood—nudged me to look closer, to question the toll this was taking on both my mental and physical health. Still, even as money was tight and stress weighed heavy, I clung stubbornly to the belief that the scale held the answer. If I could just lose a little more, tone a little further, maybe then my confidence would blossom. Maybe then everything else in my life would fall into place.

But reaching my "ideal" physique didn't silence the noise. I became shredded, leaner than I ever dreamed possible—and yet the internal battles raged on. Happiness didn't arrive with visible abs. Confidence didn't automatically seep into the places I still felt unworthy. Eventually, something inside me cracked open, a sobering reminder that health had to come first. I couldn't keep pretending. And as I looked around at the path I was carving—one day hoping to guide others in their own journeys—I felt the weight of responsibility pressing against me. If authenticity and integrity were values I claimed,

CHAPTER NINE

then I had to embody them. I had to lead by example, not by illusion.

THE CONSTANT PRESSURE TO maintain a perfect, paper-thin body began to feel hollow, even toxic. I knew there had to be another way—some balance between strength and health, a way to keep the muscle I had fought for without starving my body of its most basic needs. More than anything, I wanted my period back. It wasn't an easy decision. I had gone off birth control when I turned twenty, unwilling to continue the cycle of pills that had been prescribed to "fix" my amenorrhea as a teenager. Back then, the medication had done little more than mask the problem, leaving me with side effects I couldn't tolerate. This time, I didn't want a band-aid solution. I wanted my body to heal itself.

After months of reading and weighing my options, I finally made an appointment with my doctor and requested lab work. I was determined to approach this holistically. I began incorporating natural supplements into my routine and, perhaps more dauntingly, scaled back my training. I cut cardio. I eased up on the intensity. For someone whose identity had become so tightly wound around discipline and routine, it felt like tearing away a part of myself.

The hardest part, though, was the weight gain. My self-worth had been tethered to my reflection for so long that even the smallest changes in my body sent me spiraling. Some days I stared into the mirror, convinced I looked bigger than I was. Other days, I cried over the softness returning to my frame, mourning a body I had sacrificed so much to build. And yet, deep down, I knew this was what healing required. It wasn't about letting myself go—it was about letting myself live.

After months of steady effort, my body finally responded. Four months after I committed to change, my menstrual cycle returned. The timing struck me—it had taken almost exactly the same length of time without a period for it to come back. I hadn't put on much weight, just enough to restore balance and keep an athletic look, which mattered to me. But what mattered more was the quiet confirmation that my body was healing. My hormones were recalibrating, even the hunger hormones that had been thrown wildly off balance. The hunger was relentless. No matter how much I ate, I rarely felt satisfied. It was as if my body was asking me to repay a debt for all the years I had denied it. At first, that constant hunger unsettled me, but I chose to trust the process—nourish, rest, repeat. My body was doing the work of repair.

At the same time, I was facing another battle: the one in my mind. Body dysmorphia still whispered that I was losing ground, that I was slipping back into softness, that I was failing. Negative self-talk resurfaced in waves, pulling me into old patterns of shame. But little by little, my goals began to shift. I no longer craved the razor-sharp shredded look. Instead, I wanted strength. I wanted to build muscle, to step into the gym and feel powerful rather than fragile.

I sought out women who weren't just chasing the stage or perfection, but who were wrestling with the same body-image demons I was. Hearing their stories made me feel less alone, and their honesty gave me permission to be gentler with myself. Gradually, the habits that had bound me—restriction, overtraining, obsessive control—began to loosen their grip. My disordered eating started to fade, though a fear lingered, especially

CHAPTER NINE

around foods that weren't "clean" or whole. That fear reminded me how far I had drifted from the balance I had once wanted.

Looking back now, I see that season for what it was: not failure, but part of the path. Every setback, every fear, every pang of hunger was a step I had to walk through in order to heal. The obstacles weren't detours—they were the very road that led me here.

MY JOURNEY with mental health and body image became an invitation to look beneath the surface—into my subconscious fears, old traumas, and the shadows I had carried for years. In a world dominated by social media influencers and glossy portrayals of "wellness," it was far too easy to get swept up in curated perfection. But I didn't want to rely only on filtered images and surface-level advice. I poured money and time into learning from respected leaders in the wellness space, subscribing to programs and tuning into webinars, both free and paid. Each one offered me another perspective, another fragment of insight into health, nutrition, and human behavior. The deeper I went into my own journey, the more curious I became about why we make the choices we do. I started noticing patterns not just in myself, but in the broader culture. Every new diet trend that emerged sparked questions for me: What motivates people to embrace this? What fears or desires lie beneath it? When I tested any new approach myself, I treated it like an experiment, tracking my progress over weeks or months before deciding if it truly worked for me. Through this trial and error, I began piecing together strategies not only to survive a diet, but to sustain one long term.

But behind all that research and discipline, my relationship with food was fraying. Restriction had become my normal. I meticulously tracked every calorie and macro, allowing myself just one "cheat meal" a week. What looked like control on the outside was actually a prison. My mind was consumed by food—what I could eat, what I couldn't, what I was already planning for my next "allowed" indulgence. When the cravings became unbearable, I turned to Muckbang videos—watching strangers gorge themselves on foods I wouldn't let myself touch. It was a temporary coping mechanism, but it backfired. Each time, I ended up overeating, caught in the same vicious cycle I thought I was escaping. I told myself the problem wasn't the restriction but my lack of willpower. I refused to admit that my strict rules were fueling the binges. The aftermath was always the same: bloated, puffy, disgusted with myself. I would spiral into shame, berating my lack of discipline, convinced that I was my own worst enemy.

As time went on, I began to see the truth hiding beneath all my shifting diets and rigid routines: they weren't just about health. They were distractions, ways to avoid facing the deeper fears that lived inside me. The constant cycle of control and collapse left me mentally and emotionally drained, and somewhere along the way, I started to feel like a fraud. Imposter syndrome crept in whenever I spoke about fitness, whenever I advocated for health, because I knew the demons I wrestled with behind closed doors. Demons that felt impossible to conquer. There wasn't a single lightning-bolt moment that changed everything. Instead, there was a quiet, growing pull to go deeper. To ask myself what I was really searching for in all of this.

In that reflection, I realized something I had never admitted to myself before: my obsession with control came from somewhere else entirely. From trauma. From moments in my past when life had felt unpredictable, unsafe, unsteady. Fitness became the one place where I could reclaim control. I could track the numbers, plan the workouts, dictate the outcome. It was my safe haven—but also my trap. Because even in the midst of progress, doubt followed me like a shadow. No matter what I achieved, I hated the reflection staring back. No matter how hard I worked, I was impatient for results. And no matter how much I tried to focus on my own journey, I was always comparing myself to the fitness professionals and influencers who seemed untouchable. My self-worth had become tethered to my body. And with every step I took to fix it, the pressure only grew heavier, feeding the cycle I longed to escape.

CHAPTER TEN

ROCK BOTTOM COMEBACK

2018 was supposed to be my comeback year—the one where everything I had sacrificed finally paid off. Instead, it became the year I hit rock bottom. I had carved out the "perfect" body I had spent years chasing. And yet, inside, I felt hollow. No matter how many hours I pushed myself in the gym, my personal life was unraveling. I had buried my problems under macros and training schedules, but now they were clawing their way back to the surface, threatening to consume me.

I was alone in it all. Alone in the gym. Alone with my thoughts. Alone with emotions I had never learned how to process. Growing up, I had been taught to swallow my needs, to silence my feelings, to believe no one cared to hear them anyway. But now, as thirty crept closer, I couldn't ignore the truth: I had put so much of my life on hold, chasing an ideal that never seemed to deliver what it promised.

Seeking help did not come naturally to me—it was never modeled in my family. So when I finally dared to research therapy, fear and skepticism shadowed every click. Still, I booked an appointment. While I waited for my first session, I sat at home and made a list of everything weighing me down: the body image issues I couldn't shake, the lack of purpose, the suffocating tension of living with a mother I didn't even enjoy being around. The list felt endless. Turning thirty only added to the pressure, amplifying the fear that time was running out. Something needed to change—I knew that much. What I didn't know was if therapy could touch the broken places I had spent my whole life trying to outrun.

ARGUMENTS with my mother became the background noise of my life—loud, repetitive, exhausting. Each fight left me feeling more trapped, more certain that something inside me was missing. I craved passion, direction, purpose—anything that would make me feel alive. Instead, I was left asking myself the same haunting questions every day: *What am I doing here? Shouldn't I have my shit together by now?*

I wanted to help others, to make a difference, but I had no idea how to bridge the gap between where I was and where I longed to be. That gap was a constant ache. Therapy was both daunting and strangely comforting. Sitting across from someone whose full attention was fixed on me felt almost unbearable at first. The way my therapist studied my body language, the way she noticed the shift in my voice—it unnerved me. I wasn't used to being seen so clearly. My whole life I had played small, smoothing over conflict, putting others at ease while quietly silencing myself. To have someone reflect me back to myself was disorienting. And yet, it was also liberating. For once, I didn't have to disappear. As the sessions went on, small but noticeable changes began to surface. My therapist introduced me to a word I had never considered before: fawning. She helped me see how often I sacrificed my own needs, twisting myself into whatever shape would keep the peace, all to avoid discomfort or rejection. It stung to recognize myself in that pattern, but it also felt like a thread being pulled loose.

She challenged me to take up space. To let my truth be heard, even if it made someone else uncomfortable. It was terrifying—but also, for the first time in a long time, it felt possible.

Outside the therapist's office, I still felt unmoored. The work we did together was like training for a new fitness program—helpful, structured, full of potential—but once I left the session, it was up to me to put it into practice. And sometimes, despite everything I was learning, I fell right back into old patterns. Fear, habit, and muscle memory pulled me toward the familiar: sacrificing my own needs to keep others comfortable, willing to shrink if it meant avoiding rejection. But the more I lived this way, the harder it became to ignore the sadness simmering beneath it. Anger, too. I couldn't stop noticing how little was given back to me in return. While others seemed to effortlessly receive love, attention, and care, I was left grieving over what felt withheld from me—as if some essential part of life had been rationed out unfairly and I had drawn the short straw.

Even simple visits with loved ones carried a bittersweet weight. I left those moments not just with memories, but with questions: replaying conversations, dissecting their tone, measuring the gap between what I had hoped for and what was actually given.

Books became my companions in those years. I leaned on them for wisdom I felt I lacked, as though intelligence and emotional maturity were qualities I had to borrow from someone

CHAPTER TEN

else's pages. Beneath that, though, was a deep hunger—for self-awareness, for language to describe the things I couldn't yet name. So when I discovered personality systems like the Enneagram and Myers-Briggs, it felt like striking gold. At last, a framework to make sense of myself. A way to understand why I did what I did. I devoured the material, pouring over every description and chart with the intensity of someone desperate for answers.

But what began as a breakthrough quickly slipped into obsession. I wasn't just learning about myself—I was trying to anchor my entire identity to these systems, searching for certainty in a world where I had never felt truly seen.

As I dove deeper into personality tests and therapy, I convinced myself I was finally on the path to healing. But life had a way of throwing new challenges in my direction, forcing me to face layers I hadn't anticipated. My first therapist introduced me to the idea of inner child healing, a concept that felt foreign at first but began to take shape through journaling. Page after page, I tried to reach back into the younger parts of myself, hoping that if I tended to her wounds, the rest of me might finally feel whole.

Much of my focus in those early sessions was on my relationship with my mother. I was certain she was the root of my struggles, the wellspring of my pain. But even after we moved into a new home, the dynamic between us remained taut and heavy, as if no amount of new walls or fresh paint could soften the old patterns we carried. Hungry for answers, I asked my therapist to recommend books that might help me piece together the past. One title, written by a well-known self-help author, cracked something wide open in me. At first, I told myself I was just racing the clock—trying to understand myself before time ran out. I had no idea those books would do more than explain me; they would ignite a fire in me to truly heal. With every chapter, I found myself staring into a mirror I wasn't ready for. Family mapping exercises and Internal Family Systems techniques pulled no punches, laying bare the dysfunction I had endured. It was shocking. Overwhelming. Some nights I closed the book only to feel my chest cave with grief, unable to fathom the reality I had been living in. And yet, I couldn't look away. The words both devastated me and set me free.

THE DEEPER I went into inner child healing, the more conflicted I became. On one hand, the concepts fit together perfectly, finally giving me explanations for patterns that had haunted me for years. On the other, each exercise was a raw reminder of just how wounded I still was.

When I tried journaling or visualization, my emotions often came in tidal waves—anger, sadness, even irritation. Giving myself the attention I had been denied as a child felt strangely uncomfortable, as though caring for that younger version of me was an indulgence I didn't deserve. I had been taught to shut down, to prioritize everyone else's needs above my own. So when my therapist asked me to listen to that little girl inside—the one who still felt unseen and rejected—part of me wanted to comfort her, but another part wanted her to be quiet. It was a constant battle: the desire to heal colliding with the urge to run.

At the same time, my relationship with my mother was unraveling under the weight of old dysfunctions that had been normalized for so long. She worked briefly after we moved, but the salon's poor pay and reliance on tips drove her away within a

CHAPTER TEN

few years. Without the distraction of work, the tension between us grew sharper. Anxiety, emotional turbulence, subtle manipulation, and distancing tactics became part of our daily atmosphere. It often felt as though our roles had reversed—I was the one monitoring her choices, trying to control her actions just to preserve a fragile sense of safety. The control I clung to in the gym and in my diet didn't stop at my own body; it seeped into our home, pressing down on her, suffocating both of us in the process.

Weekends became my only escape. I would drive to Chicago with my boyfriend, grasping for air beyond the four walls that seemed to echo with our dysfunction. Those trips didn't solve anything, but for a little while, they allowed me to breathe.

AT THIRTY-ONE, change came knocking again. My therapist told me she was relocating and would need to refer me to someone new. A part of me felt unsettled, but my gut whispered what I already knew—it was time. After careful research and long hours weighing my options, I chose to begin DBT therapy with a specialist who could also guide me through the other areas of healing I was hungry to explore. Her style was different from what I was used to. Unlike my previous CBT therapist, this one carried a different personality, a new rhythm, a sharper edge. It took time to adjust, to trust her process, and to let myself be stretched in unfamiliar ways.

But I knew growth required change. The path forward wouldn't look like the path behind me—and that, I realized, was exactly the point.

CHAPTER ELEVEN

FROM SURVIVAL TO SELF-DISCOVERY

Survival mode was the backdrop of my twenties. Financial strain, trauma, and the constant need to keep moving forward left me no space to breathe, let alone reflect. But entering my thirties felt different. For the first time, I wasn't just trying to make it through—I was beginning a new journey, one of healing and self-discovery. It felt like strapping into a rollercoaster I hadn't fully agreed to ride. The sharp turns and steep drops of inner work left me dizzy, exhilarated, terrified, and hopeful all at once.

Insecurities and perfectionism weren't new companions; they had been stitched into me from childhood. Not just by society, not just by the silent pressures of social media, but by the very air I grew up in. My mother's words, her cutting critiques of herself and others, seeped into me unnoticed. They formed my earliest understanding of love: that it had to be earned through flawlessness, that worth was conditional. It wasn't until therapy —and the books, the practices, the hard conversations—that I began to question this belief system I had inherited. Even now, it

CHAPTER ELEVEN

remains a daily battle: the pull of what I was taught colliding with the slow, deliberate work of unlearning.

MY RELENTLESS SEARCH for answers eventually led me to a word I had never considered before: codependency. It came to me first through *John Bradshaw's Family Secrets*, and later through *Adult Children: The Secrets of Dysfunctional Families by John and Linda Friel*. At first, the concept felt foreign, almost clinical. But as I read on, the words began to unravel something inside me. The descriptions leapt off the page: the constant caretaking, the over-responsibility for others, the difficulty identifying and expressing my own feelings. The pendulum swings between being overly nice and the internal anger I felt. It was as though someone had been documenting my life without me knowing.

How could this be? On the outside, I had always projected strength—capable, competent, independent. But inside, I was lost. Alone. My sense of happiness often tethered to whether others approved of me, cared for me, or stayed. The books made me realize that codependency wasn't just about clinging to relationships—it seeped into every corner of my life. From the coping mechanisms I used to numb myself, to the depression I fought quietly, to the way I tolerated behaviors that chipped away at me, it was all connected. Seeing it in print was both validating and devastating. For the first time, I had a name for the ache I carried. But giving it a name didn't hand me a solution. If anything, it made the mountain ahead of me feel even steeper. Change didn't come just from awareness. Untangling years of learned behaviors felt overwhelming, almost impossible. And there were moments I wondered—if I had survived this long like this, did I really want to disturb the only patterns I knew?

The more I sat with the truth, the more I realized how deeply codependency had been woven into me. It wasn't just habits or quirks—it was the result of a lifetime of subtle messages telling me I couldn't be trusted to handle my own emotions, that I wasn't capable of standing on my own two feet. I had been sheltered from responsibility, shielded from pain, treated as if fragility was my default. Instead of learning how to face my feelings head-on, I learned to suppress them—or worse, to hand them off to my mother and wait for her to fix them. It was a cycle that kept me small, dependent, and blind to my own strength.

But once I saw it for what it was, I couldn't unsee it. Recognizing my codependent tendencies with her made it clear: something had to change. It was terrifying. Every small act of independence felt like prying my fingers off a cliff's edge without knowing if there was solid ground below. But with my therapist's support, I started taking those steps—asserting myself, setting boundaries, making decisions without seeking her approval.

Each change felt like unraveling a lifetime of conditioning, thread by thread. It was exhausting. At times, it felt like for every step forward, a new challenge appeared. Yet underneath the fear and the weariness, there was a deeper knowing: this was the only way forward. If I wanted to grow, if I wanted to stand in my own life, I had to claim the strength I had always carried but never trusted.

CHAPTER ELEVEN

THE DEEPER I went into understanding the dysfunction between my mother and me, the more uncomfortable it became. Most days I lived in a constant state of exhaustion—work, workouts, and then returning to a home that felt more like a cage than a refuge. It wasn't always like this, but the weight of our unspoken frustrations made it nearly impossible to communicate. We were two women locked in a battle of self-protection, guarding our vulnerabilities instead of reaching for connection. Her need for perfection never loosened, just as it hadn't when I was a child. I still felt the sting of her disapproval, as though simply being myself would never be enough.

The pressure mounted in other ways, too. With my mother unable to work, the full burden of bills and transportation fell on me. And because she had little socialization outside our home, I became not only her provider but also her emotional regulator. It was too much weight for one person to carry. On weekends, I fled to Chicago, desperate for air. But even in those moments of escape, guilt trailed me like a shadow. I worried about leaving her alone. And when we argued, she knew exactly where to cut —reminding me how selfish I was for wanting a life apart from her.

We were caught in a cycle we couldn't seem to break: neither listening, neither expressing, just spinning in the same loop of blame and unmet needs. As much as I tried to understand her perspective, it wasn't fair. We were two adults bound together in roles that should never have been ours to carry. And deep down, I knew the truth: I couldn't live my own life—at least not fully— while ours remained so blurred, so intertwined.

CHAPTER TWELVE

LEAVING HOME

By 2020, so much of who I was had changed from just a few years earlier. The boyfriend I had dated for seven years and I finally ended things. It wasn't an easy decision—we had countless conversations and made several attempts to save what we had built. But I was no longer the same woman I had been in my early twenties when we first met. I had grown, evolved, and in many ways, outgrown the relationship. Letting him go was painful, but it was also an act of respect—for myself, for him, and for the different paths we were now meant to walk.

That ending forced me to face a deeper truth: if I was brave enough to let go of a relationship I had built nearly a decade around, I also had to find the courage to confront the other ties in my life that were keeping me small. Which is how I found myself sitting across from my mother, heart pounding, about to tell her I was leaving.

With trembling hands, I sat down across from her, the weight of my decision pressing heavy on my chest. My heart raced as I gathered the courage to speak the words out loud. For weeks I

CHAPTER TWELVE

had been planning in secret, knowing I couldn't continue living under her controlling grip, but saying it to her face made it real.

As I spoke, sweat gathered on my palms. My eyes tracked every flicker of her expression, bracing myself for the explosive reaction I had come to expect. Instead, she sat frozen, her face a mix of shock and resignation. Quickly, I rushed to reassure her—I had everything figured out, she didn't need to worry, I would take care of it all. To my surprise, she nodded. Her initial support sparked a fragile hope inside me.

But when I began gathering my belongings in the spare room, the reality of leaving hit me like a crashing wave. My chest tightened, tears stung my eyes, and yet—again—she surprised me. She offered her help, cleaning, even setting aside some of her own things for me to take. It was as if we both knew what was happening, though neither of us had the words to say it.

Our codependent bond was fraying, finally giving way. And as fear, relief, sadness, and determination swirled inside me, one truth rose above the rest: it was time to break free. Time to begin living life on my own terms.

BY MAY OF 2021, as my 33rd birthday approached, the day I had been dreaming of finally arrived: moving-in day for my very first apartment. My mother and I had spent weeks sorting through all my belongings, packing and repacking until everything we could fit was ready to be loaded into the small U-Haul I had rented. For months, I had been preparing for this moment—collecting dishes, towels, small touches to transform four empty walls into something that felt like mine. Still, nothing could have prepared me for the rush of emotion as we carried boxes out the door. My chest tightened with every step toward the truck. Excitement, fear, grief, relief—it all collided at once. This wasn't just a move. This was a breaking point, a threshold.

When I pulled up to the apartment building and walked in to receive the keys, my hands trembled as they pressed the metal into my palm. I stared down at them, the weight of their meaning almost too much to take in. For the first time in my life, I had a space that was fully mine. A home I had chosen, earned, and prepared for. I couldn't believe it was all really happening. Tears pricked at the corners of my eyes as I let the reality sink in—this moment was real. I wanted to stay there, to savor it, but time was ticking. There was still so much to do.

We hurried back to the house and unloaded everything just in time to return the U-Haul on schedule. Thankfully, a friend who knew my story—and understood the significance of this day—had offered to help. Between the three of us, the boxes disappeared into the apartment in record time. My friend even stayed behind to assemble the bed frame I'd ordered online, his quiet way of supporting me in a milestone he knew mattered.

The apartment was chaos—piles of boxes, stray bags, loose pieces of furniture—but we each carved out our roles. My mother poured her energy into the kitchen, carefully arranging every corner as if her touch might somehow linger after I was gone. It was her way of showing she cared, her way of saying she would miss me. I buried myself in the bathroom, opening boxes and lining the shelves, letting the rhythm of unpacking keep my emotions at bay.

At one point, I slipped out to pick up pizzas, a simple meal to mark a complicated day. Hours later, we finally sat down together in the empty living room. No table, no couch yet—just

CHAPTER TWELVE

three people, three paper plates, and the hum of exhaustion in the air. It wasn't glamorous, but to me, it felt sacred. The first meal in my first home.

When they finally left around nine, I stood alone in my living room and let the silence settle. This was it. My new home. My space. The air felt different—lighter, almost sacred. Gratitude and excitement flooded through me as I whispered a silent prayer into the empty room, asking for strength to handle whatever would come. That day was more than just moving in. It was a turning point, a line drawn between the life I had known and the one I was stepping into. And as I stood there, surrounded by bare walls and scattered boxes, I knew: I was ready. Ready for the challenges, ready for the blessings, ready to finally meet myself outside the shadow of anyone else.

THE DAYS that followed brought both relief and reality. I adjusted slowly to living on my own, adding small routines to make the space feel like mine. I continued my therapy sessions, doubling down on the pursuit of knowledge and self-discovery. Outwardly, it might have seemed like nothing had changed—but inside, I was transforming. Bit by bit, I was untangling myself from codependency, learning to set boundaries that once felt impossible.

What I didn't anticipate, though, was how raw it would feel to face my triggers without the familiar buffer of my mother's presence. The anxiety that once hovered quietly in the background now crept in from every corner. With no one else to tend to, no one else's emotions to manage, I was left with my own— and they demanded my attention. Separation brought relief, but it also exposed an emptiness I hadn't expected. For so long, my life had revolved around filling my mother's emotional gaps, carrying her needs above my own. Without that constant responsibility, the silence of my apartment sometimes felt deafening. It was then that I began to fully grasp something I had only skimmed the surface of before: my mother's own lifelong struggle with crippling anxiety. In understanding her, I started to understand myself.

The absence of my mother's high functioning anxiety. It had always kept me on edge, but now that it was gone, I found myself strangely missing it. My body had become so accustomed to the constant state of tension that her cleaning and constant chatter provided. Now, in the quiet of my own home, I felt an unease I couldn't quite explain. It wasn't until later that I realized I was experiencing a withdrawal from anxiety itself. As much as I wanted to break free from it, it was also a part of me that I craved.

CHAPTER THIRTEEN

JOURNEY OF HEALING

From the moment I packed my bags and moved in 2021 to the present day of 2024, I have been immersed in a journey of deep healing. These years have not unfolded the way I imagined; instead, they veered off course, demanding more of me than I ever expected. But what I lost in predictability, I gained in transformation.

It began with the weight of my upbringing, a shadow I had carried for so long that I hardly noticed it anymore. Yet once I stepped into my own space, it followed me there, pressing for attention. As I dug deeper, new layers surfaced—old fears, buried memories, suppressed emotions that had waited patiently for their turn to be faced. It wasn't that I unearthed one life-changing revelation, but rather that years of silenced pain finally found room to breathe. The process was anything but easy. Change has always unsettled me, and these years were full of it. I often felt disoriented, as though I had lost my map and was stumbling through unfamiliar terrain. My days were filled with simple routines—work, workouts, the motions of everyday life

—but socially, I withdrew. I didn't have the desire or the bandwidth for much else. Instead, I turned inward.

Nourishing my mind, spirit, and emotions became my quiet priority. Bit by bit, I learned how to create stability for myself, building an environment that supported the kind of healing I had always craved but never known.

Days blurred into nights as I sat on the couch or the floor of my apartment, meditating, breathing, and sitting in silence. For the first time in my life, I felt safe enough to let the wounds surface, and once they did, there was no stopping them. My body trembled, my spirit cracked open, and years of grief, anger, and fear poured out. It was brutal, but it was also necessary. And somewhere in the midst of the tears and shaking, a quiet sense of peace began to take root.

Living alone became both the most peaceful and the most torturous season of my life. Peaceful, because I was finally free of codependency's grip. Torturous, because without distraction, I was face-to-face with myself in ways I had never been before. It was in that stillness that a crisis crept in, one that felt like it had appeared out of nowhere. A darkness fell over me—a disorienting fog that left me questioning everything. Many would call it the Dark Night of the Soul. At the time, I didn't know what to call it. All I knew was that I felt like I was losing my mind. Religion, philosophy, psychology, distraction, addiction—people reach for many different tools when the darkness comes. For me, it was prayer and reflection. I called out to God, to the Universe, desperate for answers, desperate for stability in a season where nothing felt solid under my feet.

CHAPTER THIRTEEN

UNCERTAINTY HAS ALWAYS BEEN my greatest struggle, and this darkness magnified it. But as I searched for meaning, a new tool revealed itself. I hadn't given astrology much thought in the past, dismissing it as little more than horoscopes and clichés. But as my healing journey unfolded after 2018, astrology caught my eye in a way it never had before. By 2021, it became another layer of exploration—something I immersed myself in, studying endlessly, pulling apart charts and transits to uncover hidden patterns. It wasn't about predicting the future. It was about understanding myself, my cycles, and the rhythms of the world around me. In the midst of uncertainty, astrology offered me a language—a framework to make sense of what felt senseless, to remind me that even in darkness, there was a larger story unfolding.

I wrestled constantly with my self-concept, trying to understand myself beyond the surface. No matter how hard I tried, the pieces never seemed to fit. My thoughts and emotions contradicted one another, leaving me frustrated and unsure of who I really was or what I was meant to do. And yet, even as a child, I had always felt a sense of purpose pulsing quietly within me. I used to imagine myself standing on a stage or in front of a camera—not because I craved the spotlight or wanted to act, but because I somehow knew I was meant to be seen. To be heard. In adulthood, that urge translated not into performance but into writing. Whenever the pull became too strong, I would pick up a pen and pour my thoughts onto paper, convinced I had something worth saying. Still, shyness clung to me. The idea of attention made me uneasy, even as I couldn't silence the curiosity burning inside me. That same curiosity eventually led me to astrology. What began as exploration quickly became validation.

For so long, I had wondered if God was punishing me.

Though I was never strongly religious, I carried a quiet belief that my suffering must have been the result of something I had done wrong, some punishment I deserved. The weight of that belief was suffocating. But astrology cracked that narrative wide open. It gave me a new lens—one where struggle wasn't always punishment, but part of a larger pattern. Where pain and difficulty weren't signs of failure, but pieces of a cycle, lessons waiting to be uncovered. What I once saw only as negative began to shift into something more meaningful, even purposeful.

AT MY CORE, I have always been deeply attuned to emotions—my own and others'—in a way that feels magnified, as if everything inside me is turned up tenfold compared to the average person. Through research, I came to understand that my introverted nature wasn't something everyone experienced, and that realization sent me digging deeper into what introversion truly meant. My capacity for social interaction has always been limited. Even something as simple as running errands could leave me drained, my energy leaking away bit by bit until I felt hollow. The lively, vocal side of me would fade into silence, replaced by a stoic expression and a quiet withdrawal into my thoughts. Retreating inward was both my protection and my refuge.

Astrology gave me words for what I had felt all along. It helped me piece together the puzzle of why I moved through the world differently, and in doing so, it stripped away much of the shame I had carried for feeling "weird" or "out of place." But it also revealed the heart of a deeper conflict: my desperate desire to control how others perceived me while simultaneously craving

CHAPTER THIRTEEN

authenticity above all else. It often left me feeling like an alien among humans—longing for genuine, soul-deep connections, but constantly running into people unwilling or unable to go there. Small talk felt like nails on a chalkboard. What I wanted, more than anything, was permission to just be myself.

As I worked through my chart and reflected on its patterns, I realized how much of this tension was rooted in my upbringing. As a child, I hadn't been encouraged to live authentically—I had been taught to contort myself into something acceptable, to bury my true self under layers of shame. Astrology became a way of tapping into that forgotten inner child, finally giving her the attention and validation she had been craving all along.

This healing wasn't just about mindset—it became somatic, too. I had to create space in my body to feel safe being authentic, to inhabit myself without apology. Slowly, piece by piece, I began reclaiming that space.

I couldn't help but envy those who seemed effortlessly confident on social media, posting whatever they pleased without a second thought. I admired their ease, the way they seemed free from the constant fear of judgment that haunted me. I wished I could do the same—share without hesitation, without editing myself into something smaller or safer. For me, every post was a battle. I overanalyzed every word, every picture, every caption, weighing whether it might come across as bragging or, on the opposite end, as insecure. The stress of it all left me feeling paralyzed, caught between wanting to express myself and fearing that doing so would expose me as inauthentic.

The truth was, my emotions had always been intense—loud, unruly, and overwhelming. They made sense now, in hindsight, but at the time they only made me feel ashamed. I cringed at how big they were, how consuming. Growing up, no one taught me how to manage them. They scared me, so I did the only thing I knew how to do: I pushed them down, locked them away, and hoped they would disappear. But emotions don't vanish just because you silence them. They wait. And eventually, they demand to be felt.

CHAPTER FOURTEEN

HEALING THROUGH BOUNDARIES

Setting boundaries and learning to express my needs became essential to my healing, but they came with a storm of inner conflict. It took immense effort—and years of trial and error—to even begin practicing them in a healthy way. What I thought was "normal" frustration revealed itself as something deeper: a reservoir of anger and resentment I hadn't even realized existed. Facing it was painful, but it also lit a fire under me. That anger gave me the motivation to finally stand up for myself, to assert that I mattered.

Still, the question haunted me: would this anger ever fade? Some days it felt endless. I hated myself for how quickly my emotions boiled over, especially when it came to my mother. At the same time, I felt a flicker of empowerment each time I pushed back, a quiet strength that came from choosing myself instead of defaulting to silence.

My therapist and I had countless heavy conversations about these cycles. At times, the only way to protect myself was to cut off contact with my mother altogether. It wasn't a choice I made lightly, but stepping away brought a sense of peace I didn't know I needed. There were even moments when I questioned whether I wanted to repair our relationship at all—sometimes, space felt more healing than connection ever had. It was no longer just a mental battle of thoughts and beliefs. It was emotional, visceral, and deeply personal—an unraveling I had to walk through if I was ever going to be free.

For far too long, I struggled with a power dynamic within myself. Deep down, I craved control—not because I wanted to dominate others, but because I had spent so much of my life feeling powerless. It was as if my subconscious needed to constantly "prove" I could take charge, that I wasn't as helpless as I had once felt. So much of it lived in my childhood, in experiences I couldn't control no matter how hard I tried.

I vividly remember the years after my mother's back surgery, watching her slowly lose herself in a toxic relationship with a man who lied, gaslighted, and chipped away at her strength. For so long she had been one of the strongest women I knew, and to see her unravel under his manipulation was a shock. I wanted to help, to step in, to protect her—but I didn't know how. And in her powerlessness, I felt powerless too.

That thread ran deeper still. My earliest years were marked by parentification and control, woven into me before I had words for it. My mother's hovering, her helicopter-like grip on every detail of my life, her anxiety projected onto me as though it were my responsibility to manage. The household chaos only magnified it—she held control through her worry, and I learned to hold control by trying to keep her steady. In my own way, I became the parent, even as I was still just a child.

As my mother's health and mental state declined, she could no longer hold either her feminine or masculine energy. The

CHAPTER FOURTEEN

balance I had once relied on disappeared, and suddenly, I was left to pick up the pieces. In my twenties, I found myself stepping into the role of a parent, filling shoes that were far too big for me. At first, I used what little power I felt I had to protect myself—shielding my anger, managing my resentment, trying to keep from crumbling under the weight of responsibility I hadn't asked for. But over time, that power shifted. I began to "abuse" it—not in cruelty, but in subtle ways that allowed me to finally put myself first, to let out the resentment I had carried for so long.

It wasn't until I began doing shadow work that I saw what was really happening. I realized my mother had never been given the care she deserved either. As a child, she was pushed into a parental role before she was ready, rejected by those who were supposed to love her, denied the basic experience of being seen, heard, and nurtured. She never learned how to care for her inner world—how could she have known how to care for mine? That truth didn't excuse everything, but it shifted my perspective. I saw how unconsciously I had fallen into the same patterns. My resentment had made me critical of her actions, her choices, even of who she was as a person. I told myself I was helping her by pushing her to do better, to be stronger. But in reality, I was echoing what had been modeled for me. It was my way of clinging to control, of making sure I would never feel powerless again.

THE POWER STRUGGLE—BETWEEN mother and daughter, and between my inner self and my outward actions—remained a constant challenge for years. And even now, it's something I continue to untangle. I'm grateful for the moments of deep introspection, and for the guidance of astrology, which helped bring these patterns to the surface faster than I could have uncovered on my own. For much of my life, my mother and I tiptoed around one another, both unsure of how to navigate the shifting tides of our relationship. She has been by my side through some of my darkest moments, yet there have also been stretches of silence where we drifted apart, each left to wrestle with our own pain.

It wasn't until she began her own therapy that I fully saw the toll our fractured communication had taken on her. That realization cracked something open in me. Repairing our bond has been painstaking work—learning not only to speak, but to truly listen, and to meet each other with empathy instead of judgment. Our journey toward healing is far from finished. But with each step, no matter how small, we keep choosing to try again. And for now, that is enough.

CHAPTER FIFTEEN

ANXIETY AND CONNECTION

My anxiety had always been a quiet companion, trailing behind me no matter where I went. Some days, I managed it with healthy coping strategies; other days, I silenced it with suppression, pretending it wasn't there.

Then I met someone. Someone who, for the first time in a long time, made the fear of being alone soften. Their presence was steady, soothing—a balm to the constant hum of worry inside me. With them, I caught a glimpse of a future I had longed for, one filled with connection and possibility. But as our relationship deepened, so did the challenges. The infamous power struggle phase arrived like an unwelcome storm, and I was unprepared for it despite all the inner work I thought I had done. What began as love and comfort quickly became a mirror, reflecting back my deepest insecurities and unresolved wounds. The old abandonment fears I thought I had buried rose to the surface, amplified until they loomed over me like a tall, dark shadow I couldn't escape. The intensity was unlike anything I had ever faced before, and it forced me to confront the rawest parts of myself.

But even amidst the turmoil, I was determined to make it work. I had invested too much of myself in this relationship to walk away without a fight. Every time we hit a wall, I convinced myself that love was enough to break through it. Yet the deeper we went, the stronger my anxiety grew. It wasn't just a whisper in the background anymore—it was on steroids, roaring in my ears, paralyzing me with fear and blinding me to any way forward.

Conflict wasn't foreign to me. I had grown up in it, playing mediator during my mother's endless arguments with her partner. Back then, I had learned how to soothe, how to understand both sides, how to keep the peace. But facing conflict in my own relationship was different. This time, the stakes were personal. This time, it wasn't just about calming the storm—it was about surviving it. I tried to slip into my old role: the peacemaker, the great listener, the one who could hold space for both perspectives and offer comfort. But instead of bringing us closer, the tension only widened the distance between us. And for the first time, I felt the quiet, unsettling question rise in me: was my determination to save this relationship worth the cost of losing myself?

MY MIND WAS A TANGLED MESS, constantly chasing answers that always seemed just out of reach. In my desperation, I signed up for courses and coaches, clinging to the hope that someone, somewhere, could fix what felt broken inside me. But no matter how much guidance I received, the same thought gnawed at me: *maybe I was the problem.* If only I could be less

CHAPTER FIFTEEN

needy, less anxious. If only I could hold it together, maybe then he would stay. Maybe then it would work.

The assignments, the coaching calls, the endless self-work—at first, they only added to the noise. But over time, I began to see my life like an onion, each layer peeled back revealing something new, yet never the whole picture all at once. With every layer removed, I came face to face with parts of myself I had long avoided—especially the part that struggled to feel safe in love.

It became undeniable: before I could build something healthy with another person, I had to understand myself. My needs. My values. My voice. Therapy, off and on continued to be my refuge during this time. It was the one space where I didn't have to perform, where my doubts and insecurities could spill out without judgment. Session by session, my therapist offered me tools and reflections that reminded me it was okay to be imperfect. Okay to be messy. Okay to simply exist as I was—flawed, human, and still enough.

The dream had ended, leaving me conflicted. Part of me knew it was a step toward deeper healing and self-discovery, but another part grieved the loss, terrified of what it meant: turning inward, facing myself, addressing the flaws I had avoided for so long. I couldn't deny that my past shaped the partners I chose—those I pushed away and those I chased after, repeating cycles that drained me dry. I didn't want future love to be poisoned by old wounds, but I also couldn't escape the truth: childhood had taught me that love was disappointment, pain, and perfection always out of reach. So, I shrank. I showed up in relationships as someone small, unworthy, terrified of being truly seen. It was time to break away from that script. To pour into my own cup, even though it had always been left half empty. Choosing myself felt foreign, almost selfish, but I knew it was the only way forward.

ONE NIGHT, I stood in front of the mirror and let my gaze linger. Flaws. Imperfections. The reflection felt both painfully honest and strangely distant. My first instinct was to fix, to change, to make the image acceptable. But as I dug deeper into my research and healing practices, I discovered something startling: the root wasn't in the mirror at all. It was in my nervous system. That realization both terrified and thrilled me. Had I known this sooner, could it have spared me the anxiety, the sleepless nights, the spirals of self-doubt? Maybe. But part of me believes the timing was intentional—that I found this knowledge at the exact moment I was ready to receive it. The conflict inside me hasn't disappeared. Some days gratitude wins; other days regret whispers. But what matters most is that both have led me here—to a path of self-discovery, of growth, and of learning to inhabit myself fully, flaws and all.

For years, I lived in survival mode. My body was constantly braced for impact, locked in fight-or-flight as if danger was always around the corner. That hypervigilance became my "normal," etched into me by years of chaotic and dysregulated interactions with my mother, by the constant uncertainty of life itself. Looking back, I can see how often my body froze or shut down in the middle of her storms—how I instinctively quieted myself, hoping to steady her when she spun out of control. At the time, I didn't know that was my nervous system's way of protecting me. I had no language for regulation, no tools to bring myself back to safety. It wasn't until after moving out that I began to notice how

CHAPTER FIFTEEN

much worse my anxiety had become. Any flicker of instability—a shift in routine, a missed paycheck, even the smallest unknown about the future—could send me spiraling. The panic felt all-consuming, as if my very survival depended on regaining control.

In desperation, I turned to meditation, hoping silence might soothe me. I deleted apps, cut back on social media, anything to create a sense of calm in the chaos. But still, the anxiety gnawed at me. The loudest thought was always the same: *I am failing at life*. Every day was a tug-of-war with irrational fears and uncontrollable symptoms—my chest tightening, my breath shallow, my mind racing in loops I couldn't escape. Underneath it all was a deeper ache: the fear of being alone. Not just alone in the room, but alone in the world. It felt like abandonment pressing against my skin, convincing me I was slowly disappearing. And yet, I knew it wasn't only fear. It was also the weight of my insecurities, the quiet but relentless belief that I was unwanted, that no one would stay when I needed them most. I guarded myself even from the people closest to me, even from my mother. Vulnerability was too risky. But in the middle of my spirals, when the panic peaked and the despair hollowed me out, the truth of what I wanted was painfully simple. I didn't need someone to fix me. I just wanted someone to hold me. To hug me and whisper the words I couldn't believe for myself: It's going to be okay.

I REFUSED TO TAKE MEDICATION, not because I thought it couldn't work, but because part of me feared what it would mean if it did. If a pill could quiet the storm inside me, then maybe there really was something broken beyond repair. I couldn't bear that thought. So instead, I threw myself into the harder road—searching, experimenting, peeling back layers until I found the root cause. The pain became my fuel. Every sleepless night, every moment of panic, every rush of shame—it all pushed me forward. I told myself that if I could face the uncomfortable truths, confront the traumas I had spent years burying, then maybe I could finally feel strong. Capable. Whole. My determination not to blindly accept answers was something I wore like armor. I was proud of my unwillingness to settle. But as I dove deeper into research, I quickly found myself spiraling down endless rabbit holes. No matter the subject—trauma, attachment, body memory—it always led me back to the same truth: a dysregulated nervous system.

The more I learned, the more I recognized the echoes of my childhood in my present struggles. Growing up, I had never felt fully seen by my mother. She was always in motion, juggling a million tasks, her energy stretched thin. I craved her attention, her validation, even just a moment of being heard. Instead, I got quick check-ins, half-questions tossed in my direction before she moved on to the next thing. It left me with a wound I couldn't name at the time—a fear of abandonment, of being a burden, of never mattering enough. As my anxiety deepened in adulthood, that wound resurfaced everywhere. At work, the smallest things could send me spiraling. A coworker glancing away mid-conversation to greet someone else felt like a knife. My body tensed, my chest tightened, and a flood of subconscious thoughts told me I was being ignored, dismissed, left behind. Shame would rise, resentment would follow, and I'd want to push them away before they had the chance to leave me hanging.

It took time, and many failed attempts, to recognize these triggers for what they were: echoes of a child who had longed to

CHAPTER FIFTEEN

be seen and heard but wasn't. The trauma of being overlooked had never really left me—it just kept finding new ways to show up, demanding to be felt, until I learned how to meet it differently.

Immersing myself in free masterclasses and online groups, I chased answers for my health and anxiety wherever I could find them. With a foundation of knowledge under my belt, I experimented with tools and techniques on my own. Without a professional guide to walk me through it, I leaned on my therapist to shape our sessions around what I was learning. Together, we unpacked triggers and worked on regulating my emotions, piece by piece. It was a painstaking process—messy, humbling, and often lonely. But through it, I discovered other key teachings that pulled me deeper into an immersive season of isolation. In that solitude, I worked to reclaim something I had never truly possessed: self-love.

My heart felt like it had been shattered into a million pieces. And while life and relationships had added their cracks, I knew the first breaking came from my parents. Facing that truth was devastating. But it was also the beginning of stitching myself back together—not perfectly, not seamlessly, but stronger than before.

CHAPTER SIXTEEN

CYCLES OF GROWTH AND SETBACK

Over the past few years, my life has felt like a constant cycle of progress and regression. Just when I thought I had uncovered and resolved a deep-seated belief, something would trigger me, and suddenly I was back at square one—or so it seemed. My mother couldn't understand my sudden sensitivity. To her, it looked like weakness, as if I was falling apart over nothing. What she didn't see was that every descent into darkness became a doorway. Those dark places, though painful, held the most growth for me. They were familiar, almost strangely comforting, because they forced me to confront what I had buried. And each time I returned, I unearthed something new: another layer of truth, another fragment of wisdom, another piece of myself I had once abandoned.

> Healing, I've learned, isn't a straight path. It's a spiral, circling back over the same terrain but with new perspective each time. It's never-ending, filled with inner conflict

CHAPTER SIXTEEN

and struggle. But it is also where I've found the deepest self-discovery—the kind that reshapes not only how I see my past, but how I carry myself into the future.

Perfectionism tied to beauty reared its head again and again, pulling me into endless cycles of despair. The pressure to look a certain way had shadowed me for as long as I could remember. On the surface, I understood the value of self-care and presenting myself well. But beneath that, I could never untangle appearance from worth. Growing up, my mother's love and acceptance often felt tied to how I looked. It seeped into me like an unspoken rule: love could only be earned through perfection—by being polished, presentable, and flawless, with no visible needs or cracks. So I chased society's impossible standards of beauty, always convinced I was falling short—because of my race, because of my features, because of how easily I compared myself to everyone else. No matter what I did, or how others may have seen me, I never felt attractive. The vision in my head never matched the reflection in the mirror. Social media only magnified it, feeding me endless images of women who seemed effortlessly gorgeous, everything I thought I wasn't.

When I started my fitness journey, I thought the discipline and transformation would finally quiet the critic inside me. Instead, it only gave her a louder microphone. The healthier and fitter I became, the harsher the standards grew. It was the inner parent I had absorbed from both society and my upbringing—relentless, nitpicking, always comparing me to someone else. Compliments poured in, but they barely grazed the thick layer of self-criticism that lived inside me. I hated the pressure to be beautiful, to conform to molds carefully crafted by billion-dollar industries that thrived on women's insecurities. Yet at the same time, I craved beauty desperately—because it still felt like the only ticket to love, validation, and acceptance.

It was a cruel, exhausting game—one I didn't know how to stop playing, even as I saw how much of myself it was costing me.

Along the way, I kept running into the same contradiction: perfectionism and self-love. On one hand, I longed to love myself unconditionally, to embrace every flaw and imperfection. On the other, I was still chasing perfection in every corner of my life. This tug-of-war led me down countless paths—from mirror work affirmations to seeking a deeper relationship with God. But no matter what I tried, one truth became clear: no amount of makeup, no cosmetic procedure, no external fix could ever make me feel perfect. Perfection, I've come to realize, is a mirage. We've been conditioned to chase it, but it always stays just out of reach. Social media makes it worse, showing us carefully filtered glimpses of what looks like perfection—but deep down, we know it's not real. Even so, we keep measuring ourselves against it, letting other people's opinions dictate our worth. That's how the endless chase begins: self-hatred disguised as self-improvement, striving for a finish line that doesn't exist.

In my own journey, I devoured book after book on perfectionism, hoping to find validation for the way I thought and lived. Somewhere along the way, perfectionism became a piece of my identity. After all, society praises those who seem to have it all together, who achieve, who keep pushing. And as someone who values hard work and believes in giving my best, I was drawn to the challenge of reaching the highest levels—not for applause, but because I felt it was what I owed myself. Yet the pursuit left me drained, frustrated, and often disappointed. The standards I measured myself against were not only unrealistic, but unsustainable. Eventually, I found myself asking a new question: *Can I hold high standards without being consumed by them?*

That question became a turning point. It pushed me to reevaluate what truly matters and to choose more wisely where I invest my time and energy. I learned that lowering my standards wasn't the answer—but neither was punishing myself with impossible ones. The balance lies somewhere in between: striving with intention, but meeting myself with kindness. That's where true growth and fulfillment begin.

PERFECTION TAKES ON MANY FORMS. For years, it showed up most visibly in how I looked, but eventually I realized it had seeped into every area of my life. I was just as hypercritical of my goals, my work, and my accomplishments as I was of my reflection in the mirror. My expectations were so unbalanced that they left me either overwhelmed or defeated. The shift came when I began to reframe how I saw progress. Instead of chasing perfection, I started to imagine my goals as weights on a scale. If everything was turned all the way up, the imbalance crushed me. But if I allowed myself to slide the weights down a notch or two—not abandoning effort, but adjusting intensity—I could still move forward without depleting myself. That simple perspective gave me space to breathe, to actually accomplish what mattered most, and to sustain my progress long-term.

With this new mindset, I found myself more creative, more productive, and—most importantly—more willing to finish things. I no longer felt paralyzed by the demand for perfection. It became okay to release something imperfect into the world and allow myself room to grow. Maybe my first published book wouldn't be my best work, but that was the point: progress, not perfection. Because chasing the illusion of flawless only kept me stuck in cycles of self-criticism, never moving, never creating.

Over the years, people have labeled me as vain, assuming my love for makeup was just a mask for my insecurities. And in truth, for a long time, it was. I cared too much about what others thought of me and wasn't sure who I really was without their approval. I wore confidence on the outside while struggling with insecurity on the inside. But little by little, I began to build confidence in other areas of my life—through my work, my growth, my healing. And as that foundation strengthened, I no longer needed the mask in the same way. I began, slowly but surely, to accept myself for who I was—not perfect, but whole.

Whenever someone called me vain, I immediately translated it as an insult—as if they were calling me stuck up, shallow, or superficial. But the truth was far from that. Fashion and makeup had been a passion of mine since I was a little girl. They weren't about hiding; they were about creating, about playing, about expression. Through astrology, I finally found validation for those interests. It gave me permission to embrace them authentically, without filtering myself through the fear of others' judgments. What once felt like a flaw began to feel like a gift.

For me, fashion and makeup are more than surface-level—they're art. They're my way of showing different sides of who I am, of reflecting my moods and creativity through colors,

CHAPTER SIXTEEN

textures, and styles. They're a language of self-expression, a mirror not of perfection, but of personality. And in finally owning that truth, I began to see that embracing what lights me up—even if misunderstood by others—is its own kind of freedom.

CHAPTER SEVENTEEN
BREAKING FREE FROM PLEASING OTHERS

For so much of my life, I lived to please others. I twisted and molded myself into whatever shape I thought they wanted me to be. It was exhausting—constantly shrinking, constantly suppressing my true self. But I convinced myself I had no other choice. Being too much, too needy, too emotional might push people away. In the process, I lost myself. My own needs, my own voice, my own desires faded into the background. It seemed like the only way to be accepted was to deny who I really was.

But healing demanded something different. It meant peeling back those layers I thought were necessary for love and realizing they were only masks. It meant unlearning the beliefs that told me I wasn't enough, letting go of relationships that no longer fit, and reprogramming the patterns that kept me trapped. With each step forward, I had to release something—a belief, a behavior, sometimes even a person. Growth wasn't just about becoming someone new. It was also about saying goodbye to the versions of myself that were built on survival instead of authenticity.

CHAPTER SEVENTEEN

BUT EVEN THOUGH I knew letting go was necessary for my well-being, it still hurt. Each goodbye stirred up childhood memories where rejection had felt like a direct attack on my character. Those early wounds shaped how I saw myself and how my brain processed emotions even now. It often felt like a constant tug-of-war between honoring who I truly was and contorting myself to fit into society's expectations—by being less, by dimming my light.

Learning that it wasn't my job to change who I was in order to please others brought both pain and liberation. Pain, because it forced me to face how much of my life I had spent living small. Liberation, because it meant I no longer had to carry that burden. Still, there were periods when my sense of worth hit an all-time low. I found myself defining my value solely by my job and career. The old belief that I wasn't good enough because I didn't have a college degree gnawed at me constantly. It was unfamiliar territory—I had never struggled with this particular insecurity before—but it consumed me.

Isolation made it worse. Alone with my thoughts, the fears only grew louder. Desperate for meaning in the chaos, I turned to every resource I could find. And then, in one of my lowest moments, I broke. I begged and pleaded with God, asking if He was even listening. What happened next is hard to describe. A wave of peace washed over me, so powerful it sent chills down my spine. My chest burned with warmth as if my heart chakra had cracked wide open, flooding me with a love deeper than anything I had ever felt before. It was unexplainable, otherworldly—a direct line to something bigger than myself. A download from spirit, straight to my hotline bling. (*Sorry Drake, but this one was divine—your line could never.*)

AS I CONTINUE my journey of self-discovery, a major part of it has been repairing my relationship with my mother. She, too, has been doing her own healing, and since I moved out, she has finally had the space to confront her codependency just as I have. Together, we are learning to approach each other with more openness, curiosity, and patience.

My relationship with my father may never look the way I once wished it could. But I've learned to accept his limitations and find contentment in the genuine moments we do share. By letting go of old expectations, I can finally appreciate him for who he is, rather than grieving who he is not.

In recent years, I've revisited every layer of my past—rebuilding what was broken, releasing what no longer serves me, and reshaping what will carry me forward. Writing has become one of my greatest tools in that process, both a source of healing and a way of stepping into my purpose. And in this season of being unattached, I have found space to fully focus on myself: to prepare for the kind of life I want to share with a partner, to cultivate security within, to clear away the weight of old wounds. It has been a time of laying down foundations—strong, steady, and lasting—before constructing the beautiful house of the life I am creating. This is the work of healing: not perfection, not arrival, but building a home within myself where I finally belong.

AFTERWORD

As I write these final words, I am reminded that healing is not a straight line. It twists and circles back, asking us to revisit old wounds with new eyes. What I've shared in these pages is not the end of my story, but simply where I am today — still learning, still unlearning, still finding new layers of myself.

There are days I feel strong and grounded, and days I stumble back into old fears. But what's different now is that I no longer see those stumbles as failures. They are reminders that growth is not about perfection — it's about coming back to myself, again and again, with compassion.

If there's one thing I hope you carry with you from my story, it's this: you are not alone. Whatever battles you're fighting inside, your feelings are real and your healing matters. There is no timeline for becoming whole, no single path that fits us all. But you are worthy of love, belonging, and peace — just as you are.

Thank you for walking through these pages with me. I hope

AFTERWORD

my story offers you courage to write your own, whether on paper or simply by living it out loud.

RESOURCES & RECOMMENDATIONS

Healing is not one-size-fits-all. The following books, tools, and practices have been meaningful on my journey. I share them here in the hope that they might also support you as you explore your own path.

Books
- *Healing the Shame That Binds You* by John Bradshaw
- *Family Secrets* by John Bradshaw
- *Adult Children: The Secrets of Dysfunctional Families* by John Friel, Ph.D. & Linda Friel, M.A.
- *The Dance of Anger* by Harriet Lerner, Ph.D.
- *The Body Keeps the Score* by Bessel van der Kolk, M.D.
- *Codependent No More* by Melody Beattie

Therapeutic Approaches
- CBT (Cognitive Behavioral Therapy)
- DBT (Dialectical Behavior Therapy)
- Inner Child Work & Journaling

- Internal Family Systems (IFS)

Mind-Body Practices
- Meditation & Breathwork
- Journaling & Reflective Writing
- Fitness & Weight Training
- Nutrition & Mindful Eating

Other Tools
- Astrology & Self-Discovery Frameworks (e.g., Enneagram, Myers-Briggs, Numerology)
- Support Groups & Online Communities (focused on healing, codependency, or fitness/wellness)
- Social Media Detox / Conscious Consumption Practices

www.ingramcontent.com/pod-product-compliance
Lightning Source LLC
Chambersburg PA
CBHW022057120526
44580CB00013B/32